W9-CLO-850

THE
UNITED STATES
AND
BRITAIN
IN PROPHECY

THE UNITED STATES AND BRITAIN IN PROPHECY

People of the Western world would be
stunned—dumbfounded—if they knew! The
governments of the United States, Britain,
Canada, Australasia, South Africa would set in
motion gigantic crash programs—if they knew!
They could know! But they don't! Why?

by Herbert W. Armstrong

Everest House
Publishers   *New York*

Table Of Contents

Introduction

ASTAGGERING TURN IN WORLD events is due to erupt in the next few years. It will involve violently the United States, Britain, Western Europe, the Middle East. It's already rather late for the free world to come *awake* to the real meaning behind current world events! Why do not the world's leaders see what is coming? Why are the world's best minds unseeing—the heads of state, scientists, educators, editors, news analysts, bankers, industrialists, leaders in business and commerce? They are totally unaware! Why?

Because they have been falsely educated and deceived into closing their minds to the great causes behind world events and trends. This world has been falsely educated to ignore causes and deal with effects! Yet all the world's problems and ills are simply a matter of cause and effect. There is a *cause* that has produced strife and war; poverty, wretchedness, inequality; crime, disease, mental ills. But the leaders do not know!

World Explosion to Erupt

The world's leaders are the educated of the world. But they were not educated in BASIC TRUTHS—the foundations of right knowledge. The most necessary knowledge is not being taught! They do not know WHAT man is—or WHY! They know nothing of the purpose or meaning of life! They were not taught to distinguish the true values from the false. They did not learn the real causes—the way to peace, to happiness, to universal abundance; nor the causes of war, unhappiness, inequality, world chaos.

They know nothing of the purpose being worked out here below. Consequently, they guide humanity on a course in conflict with that purpose, wreaking havoc upon a distressed, suffering, unhappy mankind. Lacking knowledge of the way to peace, the world does not have peace. Leaders talk of peace; they profess to work for peace; they cry out for peace—while they give approval and blind acceptance to the way that produces war!

This world has simply been going the wrong *way!*

This world is giving assent to, and conferring civilization's acceptance on, THE WAYS that are the CAUSES of all the world's ills.

And now we are fast approaching the final grand smash explosion that is going to stagger the mind of man beyond the bounds of sanity. Forces are at work today on plans, programs, conspiracies, movements that soon will erupt into a world explosion of violence and chaos such as never happened before, and never will again. Men today are tampering with forces of nature they lack the prudence, knowledge, ability and wisdom to control.

In this folly of educated ignorance, it has become fashionable today and intellectually titillating to ignore the great basic cause of all things; the fact of the purpose being worked out here below, and the master plan for its working out; the invisible but Supreme Power now soon to intervene and drastically alter the course of history—before mankind blasts itself out of existence.

Unreal though it may seem to those steeped in

modern educational deceptions, some 2,500 years ago the Supreme Power of the universe inspired a man named Isaiah to quote Him, saying: "I am God, and there is none like me, declaring the end from the beginning, and from ancient times the things that are not yet done, saying, *My counsel shall stand*" (Isa. 46:9-10). The great world powers are formulating their policies— laying their plans. But the next few years will see astounding events explode in a manner very different than the nations plan! Why?

Never a Miss

Because there is the great God who says: "The Eternal wrecks the purposes of pagans, he brings to nothing what the nations plan; but the Eternal's purpose stands for ever, and what he plans will last from age to age. . . . The Eternal looks from heaven, beholding all mankind; from where he sits, he scans all who inhabit the world; he who alone made their minds, he notes all they do" (Ps. 33:10-15, Moffatt translation).

This same Eternal God said: "To whom then will ye liken me, or shall I be equal? saith the Holy One. Lift up your eyes on high, and behold who hath created these things. . . ." And again: "Behold, the nations are as a drop of a bucket, and are counted as the small dust of the balance. . . . *All nations* before him are as nothing . . ." (Isa. 40:25-26, 15, 17).

Through His inspired prophets, the great God caused to be written, some 2,500 years ago, and preserved in writing to our time prophecies filling approximately a third of the whole Bible. In them, He named every city of consequence of that time on earth—and also every nation! And He foretold precisely what would, through the years, happen to every city and every nation! In every instance the prophecies came to pass!

What was prophesied HAPPENED to Babylon, to Tyre, Sidon, Ashkelon, Ashdod, Ekron; to Egypt, Assyria, Chaldea, Persia, Greece and Rome. There has not been a miss! Those prophecies were accurate.

And now, in other prophecies, the same supreme God has foretold precisely what is going to happen to the United States, the British nations, Western Europe, the Middle East, Russia!

Best Minds — Total Ignorance

Yet the best minds in the world are in total ignorance of the unprecedented cataclysm that is about to strike. And why have these prophecies not been understood or believed? Because the vital KEY that unlocks prophecy to our understanding had been lost. That key is the identity of the United States and the British peoples in biblical prophecy.

That key has been found! We present it to those whose unprejudiced eyes are willing to see.

The events prophesied to strike the American and British peoples in the next few years are SURE!

God says: "Surely the Lord Eternal will do nothing, but he revealeth his secret unto his servants the prophets" (Amos 3:7). These colossal world events, shrinking the first two World Wars into insignificance, WILL COME, but not until the warning has been made available for those whose eyes are willing to see.

THE
UNITED STATES
AND
BRITAIN
IN PROPHECY

1

The Lost Master Key Has Been Found

THIS MAY SOUND INCREDIBLE, BUT it's true. Editors, newscasters, foreign correspondents do not understand the real meaning of the world news they report, analyze and discuss. Heads of government are utterly unaware of the true significance of the very world-shaking events with which they deal. They have no conception of where these events are leading. Incredible? Perhaps—but true!

Winston Churchill declared before the United States Congress: "He must indeed have a blind soul who cannot see that some great purpose and design is being worked out here below of which we have the honor to be the faithful servants." But he did not understand that purpose! That great purpose long ago was master-planned by the Master Mind of the universe.

There Is Purpose

It is true, though almost totally unrealized: Mankind *was* put on this earth for a PURPOSE! And the Maker

1

of mankind sent along with the human product of His making an INSTRUCTION BOOK to reveal that purpose and to guide man in happily, enjoyably fulfilling it. But the human race has rejected the revelation and the guidance and has preferred to stumble on in the darkness of its own futile reasonings.

About one-third of that Instruction Book is devoted to basic education—revealing to man the necessary foundational knowledge otherwise undiscoverable and unknowable: knowledge of what man is, why he is, where his destiny may lead, how to reach it and live happily along the way; revealing knowledge of the true values as distinguished from the false; knowledge of the way to peace, happiness, abundant well-being. In other words, the most necessary of all knowledge—the foundation on which to build discoverable knowledge.

Another approximate third of that Book is devoted to history—to those events and experiences fulfilling the master plan during the first four millennia of man's mortal sojourn, as examples for our admonition and guidance today.

And then approximately a third—grasp this!—an entire third of our Maker's revelation to mankind is devoted to prophecy—writing the history of future events before they occur. These *fore*told future events reveal the great purpose being finally worked out—being brought to its completion.

Why This Ignorance

Now see why heads of state, news analysts, and the great minds of our time do not comprehend the real meaning of world events as they are shaping up right now.

A rational and right knowledge of this great purpose, of the Creator's master plan, of where in the progression of those foreordained events we stand today, and of major happenings prophesied yet to occur—this knowledge is the essential basis for understanding the significance and true meaning of today's dynamic world news. Without this vital knowledge, none dealing in news gathering and news reporting, none responsible for government policies can understand current world happenings or where they are leading. And not one saddled with such responsibilities does know! Why?

Two reasons, primarily: 1) They have been deceived by false education appealing to the vanity of intellect into prejudicial and disdainful rejection of the divine revelation which alone can impart this understanding; and 2) the vital key necessary to unlock closed doors of biblical prophecy had been lost.

The great world powers of our time have been, and are, the United States, the Soviet Union, Great Britain, Germany, France, and other Western European nations. The missing vital KEY is simply the *identity* of these great world powers in biblical prophecy! The staggering and cataclysmic world-shaking events soon to erupt upon a shocked, stunned, bewildered world relate directly and specifically to the United States, Britain, Germany, Western Europe, and Russia.

Not knowing how and where these nations are specifically mentioned in basic and major prophecies, the educated of the world have been utterly blinded to the plain and simple meaning of prophecy. Due to this lost key more than anything else, the Bible has come to be discredited and rejected in this world's educational system. The unproved and unprovable theory of evolution has been substituted as the foundational concept which became the supposed rational approach to knowledge.

The colossal tragedy of it! Our peoples, being thus falsely and deceptively educated from little children, have, in a supposed era of advanced rationalism and enlightenment, actually been groping around in the darkness of ignorance, misunderstanding and confusion, fatally unaware of the earthshaking catastrophe into which they are being directly plunged.

Thus our peoples have forgotten and departed far from their Maker. They have shut their eyes and closed their ears to His dynamic revelation to mankind, which, to ears that can hear, thunders out the life-and-death warning to those in the responsible positions of power!

Is it too late? Have our leaders become so steeped in a deceptive false education, so stultified that they cannot be aroused from slumber? God help us now! Time is fast closing in on us!

But the all-important master key has been found!

That key is knowledge of the astonishing identity of the American and British peoples—as well as the German—in biblical prophecies. This very eye-opening, astounding identity is the strongest proof of the inspiration and authority of the Holy Bible! It is, at the same time, the strongest proof of the very active existence of the living God!

An exciting, pulsating, vital third of all the Bible is devoted to prophecy. And approximately 90 percent of all prophecy pertains to OUR TIME, now, in this latter half of the twentieth century! It is a warning to us—to our English-speaking peoples—of immediate life-and-death import. The prophecies come alive once their doors are opened by this now discovered master key! This book will open, to open minds, this hitherto closed vital third of all the Bible. No story of fiction ever was so strange, so fascinating, so absorbing, so packed with interest and suspense, as this gripping story of our identity—and our ancestry.

Through it Almighty God gives momentous *warn-*

4

ing! Those who read, and heed, may be spared unprecedented cataclysmic tragedy soon to strike. If our peoples and their governments will awaken, heed, and return to their living God, then our nations may be spared. God help us to UNDERSTAND!

2

Prophecies Closed Until Now!

O NE MIGHT ASK, WERE NOT BIBLI-
cal prophecies closed and sealed?
Indeed they were—until *now!* And
even now they can be understood only by those who
possess the master key to unlock them. But we have
reached the approximate end of 6,000 years of biblical
history. We have reached the end of an age! We are
entering, right now, the world crisis at the close of the
present civilization. We face, today, conditions such as
the world never before has witnessed. Today the big
problem is the stark question of SURVIVAL! For the first
time in world history, the weapons of mass destruction
exist which can erase all life from the earth. Chiefs of
government and world-famous scientists have been saying publicly we must adjust to living in fear of human
annihilation, with no solutions in sight.

To those prejudicially cynical toward the Bible, I

say: It is now your only hope! Science offers no solutions. The politicians and heads of government have no answers. In the Bible alone you will find the advance news of what is now certain to occur—and occur it will *before* mankind blasts itself out of existence!

But another objector might ask, are not most of the prophecies outdated Old Testament writings, addressed only to the ancient nation Israel, of no concern to us in our time? And the answer is an emphatic no! These scintillating, dynamic prophecies were, most of them, never given to ancient Israel.

A Pivotal Book

The plain truth is, these prophecies were written for our people of our time, and for no previous people or time. They pertain to world conditions of today, and could not have been understood until today.

One of the very pivotal books of prophecy is the book of Daniel. Actually, the prophet Daniel was not the author of the book known by his name. The living God was its author! The message was transmitted to Daniel by God's angel. Daniel put to writing, to be preserved until our time, what he heard.

At the very close of his book, Daniel wrote: "And I heard, but I understood not: then said I, O my Lord, what shall be the end of these things? And he said, Go thy way, Daniel: for the words are closed up and sealed till the time of the end. . . . and none of the wicked shall understand; but the wise shall understand" (Dan. 12:8-10).

So the prophecies of Daniel were CLOSED, sealed, locked up until now! But today we are living in "the time of the end." Today the "wise" do understand! But who are "the wise"? Only those who fear and obey God—and who have the master key to unlock the locked-up prophecies. God says: "The fear of the Eternal is the beginning of wisdom: a good *understanding* have all they that do his commandments" (Ps. 111:10). And even most professing "Christians" refuse utterly to do that. No wonder they can't understand.

And don't forget, the specific key that unlocks these closed doors of prophecy is the definite knowledge of the true identity of the American and British nations as they are mentioned in these prophecies.

Stop a moment and think. If the prophecies Daniel wrote could not be understood by him; if they were "closed up and sealed *till* the time of the end"—*till* the latter half of the twentieth century—as the angel said and as Daniel wrote, then they were closed to the ancient Israelites of that day; they contained no message for Daniel's time.

Think a little further.

These prophecies could not have been given to or known by the ancient Kingdom of Israel. Daniel wrote in and after the time of the Chaldean king Nebuchadnezzar's invasion and captivity of the Kingdom of JUDAH, 604 to 585 B.C. But the Kingdom of ISRAEL had *long before* been invaded, conquered, and its people moved out of Palestine—transported as slaves to Assyria—721 to 718 B.C. (II Kings 17:18, 23-24), 117 to 133 years *before* Daniel wrote. Years before the book of Daniel was written, most of the Assyrians, *with* those Israelite slaves, had migrated from ancient Assyria northwest toward Europe. How far northwest—where they finally settled—was not then known. They had become known as the Lost Ten Tribes.

But today we do know.

Today, as Daniel wrote (12:4), knowledge has indeed increased. The whereabouts of the Lost Ten Tribes is one of the ancient mysteries now cleared up. But in

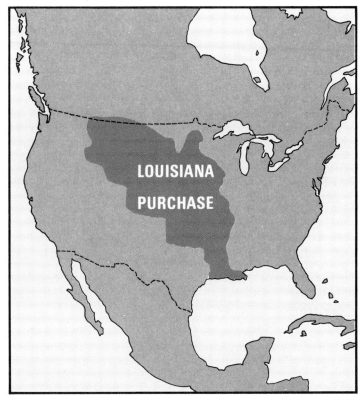

THE LOUISIANA PURCHASE—*the biggest single gain in territory for the United States. It opened up the vast Mississippi basin and put it under American control. It also included some of the best farmland in the entire world as well as rich mineral resources. The purchase facilitated further expansion to the Pacific Coast.*

Daniel's day they were lost from view—as if the earth had opened her mouth and swallowed them.

Not for Old Testament Israel

Daniel's prophecy, then, was not a message to the Old Testament Kingdom of Israel!

Now think further!

Nor was this prophecy a message for the Old Testament Kingdom of Judah. When Daniel wrote, the Jews already were slaves in Babylon. Daniel was one of the brilliant young princes of Judah, specially chosen for service in the king's palace in Babylon (Dan. 1:3-6). Daniel's strenuous duties in the Gentile king's service did not allow him to deliver this closed and sealed message to the scattered Jewish slaves. In this condition of slavery, the Jews had no system of religious meetings— no priesthood. There was no such thing as a printing press—no way to print and distribute literature. And besides, the prophecy was "closed up and sealed *till* the time of the end"—our time, now! The book of Daniel was *not* a message for the Jews of Old Testament times!

Finally realize: It is emphatically clear that these prophecies pertain to no time but to *our time,* in this twentieth century!

Then know this, further:

The greatest mystery book of the entire Bible, to most, has been the book of Revelation. But the book of Daniel is the key to the book of Revelation. And in the book of Revelation, solely and alone, do we find the world events of all prophecies correlated in order of time sequence. The book of Revelation, then, holds the key for putting together all of the prophecies in proper time order. And Revelation, too, was a closed and sealed book—until our time, now. We realize that the living Jesus is the Revelator—and that He has stripped off the seals and opened this mystery book to right understanding.

And where does that lead us? To the fact that prophecy generally was written and preserved for *our time today!* And some 90 percent of all prophecy pertains actually to this latter half of the twentieth century. And the one central master key to prophecy as a whole is the identity of the United States and the British nations in these prophecies for today!

These prophecies could not pertain to any time previous to our precarious present!

It may not be generally realized—but neither Britain nor the United States became great world powers until the nineteenth century. Suddenly, in the very beginning of the nineteenth century, these two—until then small, minor countries—suddenly spurted to national power and greatness among nations, as no nations had ever grown and multiplied in wealth, resources and power before.

By 1804 London had become the financial hub of the world. The United States had exploded out of its swaddling clothes of the 13 original states and had acquired the expansive Louisiana Purchase. It was fast sprouting up to become the mightiest nation of all time. But Britain burst forth to greatness first, and until the World Wars had become the greatest empire, or commonwealth of nations, in all history.

Could We Be Ignored?

Between them the British and American peoples had acquired more than two-thirds—almost three-fourths—of all the cultivated physical resources and wealth of the world. All other nations combined possessed barely more than a fourth. Britannia ruled the waves—and the world's commerce was carried on by water. The sun never set on British possessions.

Now think!

Could the British and American peoples be ignored in prophecies of world conditions that fill a third of the entire Bible—when some 90 percent of all those prophecies pertain to national and international world happenings of *our time, now?*

Staggering?

Indeed it is. And yet, precisely as prophesied, Britain's sun has now set. As these same prophecies that foretold Britain's greatness revealed far in advance, Britain has already been reduced to a second-rate or third-rate power in the world.

And the United States? Today America finds herself heir to just about all the international problems and headaches in this post-World-War-II, chaotic, violent world. And the United States has won her last war— even little North Vietnam held her at bay. Many other nations sap America's national strength, "and he knoweth it not," as God long ago foretold!

On the world scene nothing is so important right now as to know where the white, English-speaking peoples are identified in scores and hundreds of prophecies—prophecies which describe vividly our sudden rise to national power and reveal the causes of that greatness; prophecies that paint a crystal-clear picture of our present international dilemma; prophecies that open our eyes wide to see what now lies immediately ahead for our nations—and what our ultimate and final status shall be.

3

National Greatness Promised Israel—Yet The Jews Never Received It—Why?

PRIOR TO WORLD WAR II, THE American and British peoples had acquired more than two-thirds of the cultivated resources and wealth of the world. Yet, astonishing wonder though it be, we acquired nearly all of it rather suddenly, since the year 1800. Never in all history did anything like this occur. Never did any people or nation spread out and grow so suddenly and rapidly into such magnitude of national power.

Yet we are beholding before our very eyes the diminishing and evaporating of this national greatness, wealth and power. In the case of Great Britain, it is disintegrating even more rapidly than it developed! Britain has been almost overnight stripped of her colonies and her possessions—source of her wealth—and reduced to a second-rate or third-rate power. Why? There is a reason! It is bound up with history and divine promises pertaining to Israel. Promises never yet inherited by the Jewish people. And now, unless the people *and* the government of the United States will heed and take immediate and drastic action, the American nation is slated to go down even more suddenly to utter ignominy and loss of all national wealth, greatness and power!

And for the SAME REASON!

It behooves us without delay to quickly review that history and open our eyes to divine promises and warnings almost wholly unrealized by our peoples. It is all connected with the generally ignored plain and simple Bible story that leads to knowledge of our incredible ancestry and modern prophetic identity. And it is the most amazing, the most fascinating story you ever read. Stranger than fiction—yet it is TRUE!

Why Do We Have Israel's Bible?

Millennia ago, this same national greatness, wealth and power was promised by the Almighty to Abraham. Yet few have ever noticed this astonishing fact in Scripture. We must realize, if we would understand, a peculiar fact. The Holy Bible is the particular Book of a definite nationality—the children of Israel.

It is undeniable! Its history, from Genesis to Revelation, is primarily the history of one nation or people—the Israelites. Other nations are mentioned only insofar as they come into contact with Israel. All its prophecy, too, pertains primarily to this people of Israel, and to other nations only insofar as they come into contact with Israel. The Bible tells of these Israelites and their God. It was inspired by the God of Abraham, Isaac and Jacob, committed to writing through Israelites exclusively, and preserved until after the New Testament was written by these Israelites. In its sacred passages we read that all the prom-

14

ises and the covenants of God, all the sonship and the glory, belong solely to Israel (Rom. 9:4).

Yet we must face the astounding fact that our white, English-speaking peoples—*not* the Jews—have inherited the national and physical phases of those promises!

How could this have happened?

The Bible is an Israelitish Book, preeminently of and for the Israelitish nationality, inspired by their God through their prophets. Is it not indeed strange that we English-speaking peoples are today the greatest believers in and exponents of this Book of the Hebrew people; that of all nations we are the chief worshipers of Israel's God and Israel's Messiah—in name and in form, if not in truth and in deed?

The more these facts are realized, the more apparent it becomes that a full knowledge of these Israelites is necessary to a right understanding of the Holy Bible, which is chiefly concerned with them as a people. And this knowledge becomes important if we are to understand the present status of the American and British peoples in the world—and their relation to unprecedented world conditions at this fateful hour! Let us remember as we approach this fascinating story that the Bible is concerned with the material, the fleshly, the literal, racial and *national*, as well as with the spiritual. Let us not spiritualize away national things, nor nationalize spiritual things. Let us understand the sacred Word of God as it is!

Nation Began With One Man

Before the days of Moses there was no nation on earth known as God's particular nation. Prior to Moses there was no written Word of God; no inspired Scriptures; no Holy Bible. Think of it! For more than two thousand

15

The United States
Territories Held During

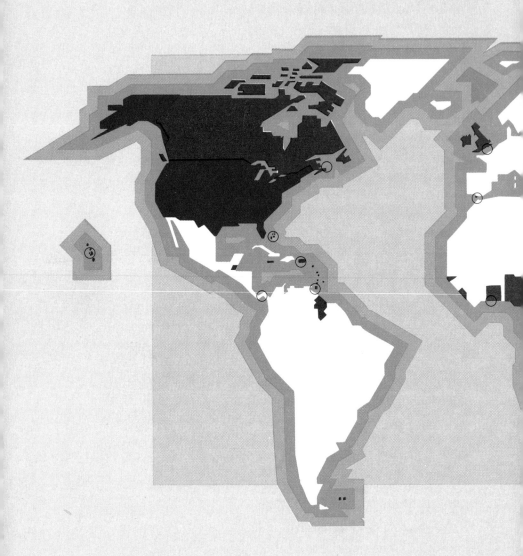

and Great Britain—
Greatest Extent of Power

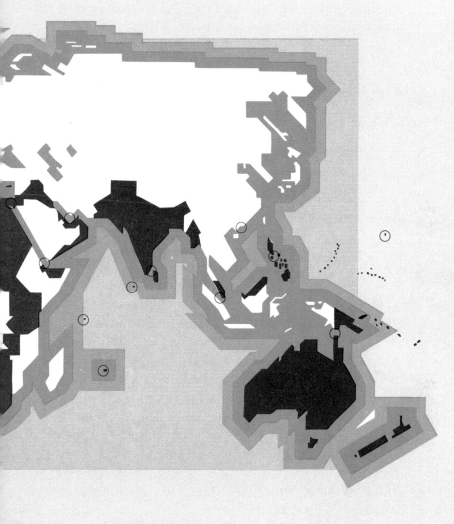

■ United States   ■ United Kingdom   ○ Land and Sea Gates

five hundred years—two-and-a-half millennia—mankind existed without any written revelation from God! The only historic record of God's dealing with mankind prior to Israel is the revealed history of the Bible. And— even more astonishing—only the first eleven of the fifty chapters of Genesis are devoted to the entire history of the world prior to Abraham, father of the Israelites!

Surprising? Only the first eleven chapters of the very first book of the Bible are used to record for us the history of the first approximately 2,000 years—more than one-third of its entire span.

God began this world with just one man—Adam. Whatever God does through human agencies must start the smallest, and, like the grain of mustard seed, grow big. To this first man God communicated directly and personally. God revealed all essential knowledge otherwise inaccessible to the human mind. The basic essentials of all knowledge—what *is* man?—WHY is he here?—what's the PURPOSE of life?—what is the WAY of life that will produce peace, health, prosperity, happiness and joy?—what is man's END—his destiny?—God revealed this basis of all knowledge to the first man.

To Adam, God revealed Himself—the Eternal Creator-Ruler of earth and all the universe. God revealed to Adam that he was, unlike animals, made in the form and shape of God with powers of mind possessed by no other physical creature; with the potential, through free choice, of developing the very character of God and of inheriting eternal life in the Kingdom of God. To Adam God revealed the way of life that would result in everything man desires: peace, enjoyable life, happiness, abundant well-being.

To produce these blessings—to be the *cause* of such desired *effect*—God had set in motion His inexorable spiritual law. But Adam listened to Satan and leaned to

18

his own human understanding. He disobeyed God, rejected the way to every desired result, and set out on the human course of greed and vanity.

Mankind Spurns God's Way

As men began to multiply on earth, Adam's sons followed in his Satan-inspired course of human nature. Prior to Abraham, only three are mentioned as accepting God's way of life—only three during more than a third of the whole span of the history of mankind. Abel was called righteous; Enoch walked with God; and Noah was a preacher of righteousness, which is simply obedience to God's government (Ps. 119:172). Aside from these three and possibly Shem, there is no record that any man prior to Abraham yielded to the rule of the Eternal.

By the time of Abraham men had lost all knowledge of the true Creator-Ruler, His revelation of His purpose, and the way of God to peace and happiness and to life eternal. Man pursued his own ways and devices, walking contrary to the spiritual laws of God. Sin and violence filled the earth.

God Started His Nation With One Man

It was in such a world, which had strayed far from God and knowledge of the glorious benefits of God's rule and the worship of the true God, that one man was honest and upright, submissive and teachable, strong and purposeful. So God gave him a test command of obedience. To this man, Abram, God commanded: "Get thee out of thy country, and from thy kindred, and from thy father's house, unto a land that I will shew thee: And I will make of thee a great nation" (Gen. 12:1-2).

Here was a command, which was a *condition* and a PROMISE, provided the condition of obedience was met.

19

And so now, as God had started the whole world with one man, He started His own peculiar nation in the world from one single man—Abraham. As the world, which has strayed far from God and the blessings of God's worship and rule, was started with one man who rebelled against God and rejected His rule, so God's own flesh-born nation, from which is to be reborn the Kingdom of God, was started with one man who obeyed God without question, and accepted His divine rule.

Did Abram stop to argue and reason? Did he say: "Let's reason this out a bit first; here I am in Babylon, in the very center of all this world's commerce, society and gaiety. Why can't you just as well give me this promise right here, where everything is pleasant and alluring? Why must I leave all this and go over to that uncivilized land?"

Did Abram quibble, resist, argue, rebel?

He certainly did not!

The inspired Scripture account states simply: "So Abram departed." There was no arguing with God. There was no human reasoning that God was all wrong. There were no foolish questions: "Why must I leave here?" "Can't I do as I please?" There was no stopping to say, "Well, here's the way I look at it."

"Abram departed." Just plain, unquestioned obedience!

And God established this man, whose name He later changed to Abraham, as the *father* of His nation, *Israel!* To Abraham and his descendants were all the promises of God made. And we must become like Abraham, and through Christ one of his children, if we are to inherit the promise of eternal life in God's Kingdom.

Of His peculiar flesh-born nation, Israel, the Eternal said: "This people have I formed for myself; *they shall* shew forth my praise" (Isa. 43:21). That prophecy shall yet—and soon—be fulfilled!

Dual Promises to Abraham

Few have realized it, but a duality runs all the way through the plan of God in working out His purpose here below.

There was the first Adam, material and carnal; and there is Christ, the second Adam, spiritual and divine. There was the Old Covenant, purely material and temporal; and there is the New Covenant, spiritual and eternal. God made man mortal, physical, of the dust of the ground and of the human kingdom; but through Christ he may be begotten of God to become immortal, spiritual, and of the Kingdom of God.

And in like manner there were two phases to the promises God made to Abraham—the one purely material and national; the other spiritual and individual. The spiritual promise of the Messiah, and of salvation through Him, is well known by the most superficial Bible students. They know that God gave the spiritual promise to Abraham of Christ to be born as Abraham's descendant—and that salvation comes to us through Christ. But—and this will sound unbelievable, yet it is true—almost no one knows what that salvation is; what are the promises of salvation we may receive through Christ; how we may receive them, or when—incredible though that sounds! But that truth belongs in another book.

What is essential to the theme of this book is the fact that God also made another entirely different, most amazing national and material promise to Abraham which has been almost entirely overlooked.

Notice now again how God first called Abram, and the *twofold* nature of His promises: "Now the Eternal had said unto Abram, Get thee out of thy country, and

Plain Truth Photo

GIBRALTAR, *the strategic western "gate" to the Mediterranean, stood for three centuries as the symbol of Britain's far-flung power. Today it is one of the Empire's few remaining vestiges.*

from thy kindred, and from thy father's house, unto a land that I will shew thee: And I *will make of thee* A GREAT NATION. . . . and in thee shall all families of the earth be blessed" (Gen. 12:1-3).

Notice the twofold promise: 1) "I will make of thee A GREAT NATION"—the national, material promise that his flesh-born children should become a great nation—a promise of RACE; 2) ". . . and in thee shall all families of the earth be blessed"—the spiritual promise of GRACE. This same promise is repeated in Genesis 22:18: "And in *thy seed* shall all the nations of the earth be blessed." This particular "one seed" refers to Christ, as plainly affirmed in Galatians 3:8, 16.

Right here is where those who profess to be "Christians"—and their teachers—have fallen into error and scriptural blindness. They have failed to notice the twofold promise God made to Abraham. They recognize the messianic promise of spiritual salvation through the

22

"one seed"—Christ. They sing the hymn *Standing on the Promises*—falsely supposing the *promises* to be going to heaven at death.

This is a pivotal point. This is the point where professing "Christians" and their teachers jump the track of truth. This is the point where they switch off the track that would lead them to the missing master key to the prophecies. They miss the fact that God gave Abraham promise's of physical RACE as well as spiritual GRACE.

But the plain fact that the "great nation" promise refers alone to race—not the "one seed" of Galatians 3:16, who was Jesus Christ the Son of Abraham and the Son of God, but to the plural, multiple seed of natural fleshly birth—is made certain by God's repetition of His promise in greater detail later.

Notice carefully! Understand these promises!

"And when Abram was ninety years old and nine, the Eternal appeared to Abram, and said unto him, I am the Almighty God; walk before me, and be thou perfect. And I will make my covenant between me and thee, *and will multiply thee exceedingly. . . . thou shalt be a father of* MANY NATIONS. Neither shall thy name any more be called Abram, but thy name shall be Abraham; for a father of MANY NATIONS have I made thee" (Gen. 17:1-5).

Notice, the promise is now conditional upon Abraham's obedience and perfect living. Notice, the "great nation" now becomes many nations—more than one nation. This cannot refer to the "one seed," Christ. The following verses prove that.

"And *I will make thee exceeding fruitful*, and I will make *nations* of thee, and *kings* [more than one] shall come out of thee" (verse 6). Notice, these nations and kings shall *come out of* Abraham—physical generation—multiple seed, not just one descendant *through whom* scattered individuals *may* become Abraham's children by spiritual begettal through Christ (Gal. 3:29). The scattered, individual Christians do not form NA-TIONS. The Church, it is true, is spoken of as "a royal priesthood, an holy nation" (I Peter 2:9), but Christ's Church is not divided into "many nations." This is speaking of race, not grace.

"And I will establish my covenant between me and thee and thy seed after thee in *their* generations . . ." (Gen. 17:7). The "seed" is plural—"in their genera-tions." "And I will give unto thee, and to thy seed after thee, *the land* wherein thou art a stranger, all the land of Canaan [Palestine], for an everlasting possession; and I will be THEIR God" (verse 8).

Notice, the land—material possession—is promised to the plural seed, of whom He is "their," not "his," God. The plural pronoun "their" is used again in verse 9: "and thy seed after thee in *their* generations."

But now examine this PROMISE carefully!

The future of great nations rests on the promises the eternal Creator made to Abraham. The only hope of life after death for anyone—regardless of race, color or creed—is dependent on the spiritual phase of these promises to Abraham—the promise of grace through the "one seed"—Christ the Messiah!

How Much Land — What Size Nations?

These are not casual, incidental, unimportant promises. These are basic—the foundation for the establishment of the greatest world powers; the basis for any personal salvation spiritually; for any hope of eternal life for humans. These are stupendous promises. The future of mankind is based, by the Creator God, on them.

Jesus Christ came "to confirm the promises made

unto the fathers" (Rom. 15:8)—Abraham, Isaac, and Jacob.

A carnal cynic, whose mind is hostile to God and His promises, purposes, and ways, tosses these tremendous promises aside, saying flippantly, "Oh yeah?—but what kind of 'many nations'? Twentieth-century style? Nations of 100 million or more people? Don't be ridiculous! Those men who wrote the Bible knew nothing of nations that would be 'great' by our twentieth-century standards! They referred only to little nations like there were then—nations containing no more people than a small township or county today!

"And then how much land did this promise include? Was God supposed to have promised an inheritance out of the land of Canaan, as mentioned in verse 8 of Genesis 17? And then in repromising this land to Jacob, all the land that was included was 'the land whereon thou liest' in Genesis 28:13. How much land was that? Not more than a tiny plot two feet wide, and about six feet long!"

A cynical objector actually argued thus!

So let's answer the sneering closed-minded cynic! Let's check carefully, and see precisely what was promised under this phase of the promises pertaining to race—the physical, material, national promises. I leave the checking of the spiritual phase of the promises to be explained in other booklets or articles.

How much land was promised?

A Cynic Argues

But first hear out the refutation of the criticizing cynic. "That promise," continues the objector, "of 'many nations' was written in Hebrew, and the Hebrew word for 'nation' is *goi*, and for more than one, plural, it is *goiim*. It merely means some people—it could mean just a little

25

handful of Abraham's children and grandchildren."

I mention this because a self-professed "scholar" did one time make this very ridiculous statement and professed to reject this entire important truth on these arguments primarily. If the reader cares to check up on this Hebrew *goi* he will find it means "nation"—or, in the plural, "nations" or "peoples," without regard to size of population. This is the word most often used—actually hundreds of times in the Old Testament—for the various nations of the world, including the largest nations. In the prophecy of Joel 3, verse 2, God says He will gather "all nations." That is speaking of a time yet future, in this twentieth century—and the Hebrew *goiim* is used. There the word *goiim* includes such nations as Russia, Germany, Italy, China, India—pretty big nations.

But God promised that Abraham's literal, human, flesh-and-blood descendants should become "a *great* nation" (Gen. 12:2); that He would "*multiply thee exceedingly*" (Gen. 17:2); that "thou shalt be a father of *many nations*" (verse 4); and that "I will make thee *exceeding fruitful*, and I will make *nations* of thee" (verse 6). As we proceed along with other promises and prophecies, we shall see that biblical language describes these as great and large nations.

And how much land? In Genesis 17:8, God promised "all the land of Canaan," but in other scriptures He promised much more. In Genesis 15:18: "In the same day the Eternal made a covenant with Abram, saying, Unto thy seed have I given this land, from the river of Egypt [the Nile] unto the great river, the river Euphrates." The Euphrates is a considerable distance to

---

THESE TWO GATES *control the long sea passage from the western Mediterranean, through the Suez Canal to the southeastern end of the Red Sea. Britain now controls only Gibraltar.*

Hunting, Freibergs—Ambassador College

27

the east in the ancient land of Babylon, which is today Iraq—considerably east of Palestine.

But all of this objector's arguments are refuted and made ridiculous by the very next verse from the one he quoted when he said that all that was promised was a plot about 2 x 6 feet. He could have read this next verse: "And thy seed shall be as the dust of the earth, and thou shalt spread abroad to the west, and to the east, and to the north, and to the south" (Gen. 28:14).

Here the size of the "many nations" is compared to the number of grains of dust of the earth. Elsewhere God compared the populations of these promised nations to the grains of sand on a seashore and to the stars—uncountable for multitude.

As we proceed, the magnitude and the reality of these promises will become quite evident.

Not Fulfilled in Jews

Again, notice carefully—the Jews have never been more than one nation. They are not, and never have been, many nations. So here is an amazing prophecy, a solemn promise from Almighty God, that could not be fulfilled in Christ, in Christians, nor in the Jews. We must look for a number of nations apart from either the Church or the Jews. Amazing as it is, we must do it or deny God's promise!

God put Abraham to the test, and Abraham, through faith, obeyed—even to being willing to sacrifice his only son, if need be. And after that the covenant no longer was conditional. Now it became UNCONDITIONAL.

"By *myself have I sworn*, saith the Eternal, for BECAUSE thou *hast done* this thing, and hast not with-

HONG KONG on the coast of China is a key to trade in the area. The Khyber Pass, today in Pakistan, controlled the entrance to the subcontinent of India. Both were in British control.

Jorgenson—Ambassador College, Blackhawk Films

held thy son, thine only son: that in blessing I will bless thee, and in multiplying I will multiply thy seed as the stars of the heaven, and as the sand which is upon the sea shore; *and thy seed shall possess the gate of his enemies* [or, as correctly translated in the Revised Standard Version, "And your descendants shall possess the gate of their enemies." The Fenton translation renders it: "And your race shall possess the gates of its enemies"—so far the material, national promises of race]; and in thy seed [Christ] shall all the nations of the earth be blessed [this promise is spiritual, of grace]; because thou hast obeyed my voice" (Gen. 22:16-18).

The promise now is UNconditional. God has sworn to make it good. God does not promise these things IF Abraham or his children do certain things. He promises them to Abraham BECAUSE he already has performed his part of the agreement. If these promises could be broken or annulled, then no promise in the Bible is sure!

These promises cannot be broken or annulled. Not if it be true that "heaven and earth shall pass, but my word shall NOT pass away." Now God must perform His part without fail.

Notice an additional detail of the promise—the nations who are Abraham's racial descendants are to possess the gates of their enemies. A gate is a narrow passage of entrance or exit. When speaking nationally, a "gate" would be such a pass as the Panama Canal, the Suez Canal, the Strait of Gibraltar. This promise is repeated in Genesis 24:60 to Abraham's daughter-in-law: "Be thou the mother of thousands of millions, and let thy seed possess the gate of those which hate them."

Notice, Abraham's descendants would possess vital geographic passageways of their enemies—"those which hate them." This has never been fulfilled in the Jews, nor could it be fulfilled after Jesus Christ returns to rule the nations and establish world peace. This promise could only be fulfilled in the present world or else we must deny the Bible as God's revealed Word. We must look for a people forming more than one nation—yet all one people, children of Abraham—either now or in history who possess the sea gateways of the world, or we must deny the Word of God. It is a test of the inspiration of the Bible and of God's power to rule this world!

A Nation and a Company of Nations

These tremendous promises were repromised to Isaac and to Jacob. Ishmael and Abraham's other sons were rejected from this birthright. Esau, Isaac's son and Jacob's twin brother, sold it and was rejected. The promise, as confirmed to Isaac, is recorded in Genesis 26:3-5: "I will be with thee, and will bless thee; for unto thee, and unto thy seed, I will give all these countries, and I will perform the oath which I sware unto Abraham thy father; and I will make thy seed to MULTIPLY *as the stars of heaven,* and will give unto thy seed all these countries. . . ." Notice! Twice God promised "all these countries." That is millions of times larger than the 2 x 6-foot plot our "intellectual" cynic contended for. Also, Isaac's descendants were to "MULTIPLY as the stars of heaven." That's thousands of times larger than a tiny "township."

To Jacob it is repeated in Genesis 27:26-29, where MATERIAL blessing of wealth in the things of the ground is added, with the prophecy that heathen nations shall be ruled by the birthright nations of Israel. "Therefore God give thee of the dew of heaven, and the fatness [margin: fat places] of the earth, and plenty of corn and wine: Let people serve thee, and nations bow down to thee: be lord over thy brethren, and let thy mother's sons bow down to thee: cursed be every one that curseth thee, and blessed be he that blesseth thee."

To Spread Worldwide

And we find the promises again in Genesis 28:13-14, where the added detail that these nations of Israel shall eventually spread around the world is recorded. "And, behold, the Eternal . . . said, I am the Eternal God of Abraham thy father, and the God of Isaac: the land whereon thou liest, to thee will I give it, and to thy seed; and thy seed shall be as the dust of the earth, and thou shalt spread abroad to the west, and to the east, and to the north, and to the south. . . ."

The original Hebrew for "spread abroad" means "to break forth." This promise places no limit on how far east, west, north and south Jacob's descendants should spread. Thus it indicates they would spread around the earth. This is confirmed in Romans 4:13: "For the promise, that he [Abraham] should be the heir of the world. . . ."

But this is not a promise that Abraham's descendants should inherit, own, and possess the whole of the earth, leaving nothing for Gentiles—that is, prior to the new earth—but rather that, in years and centuries to come, they would spread and occupy certain areas in various parts of the earth. Yet, the new earth—after the millennium—will be inhabited only by those who shall be Abraham's children through Christ (Rom. 4:13).

There is a phase of this prophecy heretofore utterly overlooked—not before understood. Indeed these birthright Israelitish nations *have* spread to and occupied various lands or areas in many locations around the world. This occurred after they were—721-718 B.C.—driven in a captivity out of their own promised land of Samaria in Palestine. The next verses in Genesis 28 complete this phase of the prophecy. "And, behold," God continued, "I am with thee, and will keep thee in all places whither thou goest [God is here referring, not to Jacob personally, but his descendants who were to spread abroad in all directions], and will bring thee again into this land; for I will not leave thee, until I have done that which I have spoken to thee of" (verse 15).

This generally unnoticed, but significant prophecy will be fulfilled at the second coming of Christ. It is explained further in Jeremiah 23:7-8, and 50:4-6, 19-20, and other prophecies.

Repromised to Jacob

Still later, God appeared to Jacob, whose name was changed to Israel, even further defining the makeup of these "many nations" thus: "And God said unto him, I am God Almighty: be fruitful and multiply; A NATION and a COMPANY OF NATIONS shall be of thee, and kings shall come out of thy loins" (Gen. 35:11). The Moffatt translation renders it "a nation, [and] a group of nations." The Fenton rendering is "a nation and an Assembly of Nations." The RSV translates it as in the Authorized Version, above quoted. So the "many nations" are eventually to take shape as a nation—one great, wealthy, powerful nation—and another company of nations—a group, or commonwealth of nations.

Mark carefully this crucial fact! This is basic, if you are to grasp the all-important key to all prophecy—the very key to the real meaning of the unprecedented world events of the present. This promise never has been fulfilled in the Jews. It cannot be "spiritualized" away by interpreting it as being inherited only through Christ. It could not pertain to the Church, for there is but one true Church acknowledged in the Bible, and it is not a nation, or a group of nations, but one Church of called-

33

out individuals scattered through all nations. Yet this amazing promise MUST stand fulfilled, unless we are to deny the Bible and God's sacred Word!

Here is the enigma of the ages! Is this a divine promise unkept? Thomas Paine and Robert Ingersoll lost faith in God and rejected the Bible because they believed these national promises were never fulfilled.

The very fate of the Bible as the revealed Word of God—the evidence of the existence of God—hangs on the answer to this momentous question. The Jewish people did not fulfill these promises. The promises do not refer to the Church. The world with its great church leaders does not know of any such fulfillment. Did God fail? Or has He made good this colossal promise unknown to the world? The true answer is the most astonishing revelation of Bible truth, of prophecy, and of unrecognized history!

4

The Separation Of The Birthright And The Sceptre

NOW WE COME TO A MOST VITAL distinction, and a bit of Bible truth known to but a very few. Very few, indeed, have ever noticed that the promises to Abraham were twofold. But the Bible itself makes sharp distinction between these two phases of the promises.

The spiritual promises—the promises of the "one seed," Christ, and of salvation through Him—the Bible calls the *sceptre*. But the material and national promises relating to many nations, national wealth, prosperity and power, and possession of the Holy Land, the Bible calls the *birthright*.

Race, Not Grace

Let us understand the meaning of the terms:

"*Birthright*: native right or privilege"—*Standard Dictionary;* "any right acquired by birth"—*Webster's.* A birthright is something which is one's right, by birth.

It has nothing to do with grace, which is unmerited pardon and a free gift which is *not* one's right. It has to do with *race*, not grace. Birthright possessions are customarily passed down from father to eldest son.

"*Sceptre:* kingly office; royal power; badge of command or sovereignty"—*Standard Dictionary.* The promised kingly line culminates in *Christ,* and involves *grace* to all.

We have seen how both sets of promises, right of birth and gift of grace, were unconditionally made by God to Abraham. Both the birthright and the sceptre were repromised by the Eternal to Isaac and to Jacob. But the fact that should open your eyes, as a joyous truth newly discovered, is that from that point these two sets of promises became separated! The sceptre promises of the kingly line culminating in Christ, and of grace through Him, were handed on to JUDAH, son of Jacob and father of all Jews. But the astonishing truth is that the birthright promises were never given to the Jews!

Let that be repeated! Realize this! The birthright promises were never given to the Jews!

Turn to these passages—read them in your own Bible!

"The sceptre shall not depart from Judah..." (Gen. 49:10).

"...But the birthright was Joseph's" (I Chron. 5:2).

Of course it is well understood that the sceptre went to Judah and was handed down through the Jews. King David was of the tribe of Judah. All succeeding kings of David's dynasty were of the House of David, tribe of Judah. Jesus Christ was born of the House of David and the tribe of Judah.

Another eye-opening truth completely unrealized by most people today is the fact that only a *part* of the "children of Israel" were Jews.

36

Read that little understood fact again!

The full explanation and proof of this must be reserved for Chapter VI. *Only* those of the three tribes of Judah, Benjamin and Levi were Jews. While all Jews are Israelites, most Israelites are *not Jews!*

So understand! The birthright promise *did not* pass on to the Jews! But the sceptre—the promise of *Christ* and of *grace*—was passed on to the Jews! "Salvation," Jesus said, "is of the Jews"! (John 4:22.) "The gospel of Christ," wrote Paul, "is the power of God unto salvation to every one that believeth; to the JEW *first*, and also to the Greek" (Rom. 1:16). The promises of *grace* were handed down through JUDAH!

But the promises which the Bible terms the "birthright" have not been understood at all. Few have ever noticed that God made any promises to Abraham other than the sceptre. Few know what is in the Bible!

Birthright Never Given to the Jews

Fewer still have understood that these great national material promises were never given to the Jews! The astonishing and vital fact that many have overlooked is "the birthright is JOSEPH'S." And, as we shall see later, neither Joseph nor his descendants were Jews! Astounding as it may be, it's true!

This knowledge about the birthright is the pivot of this entire truth which will prove *the key* to the understanding of all prophecy! It's of supreme importance that you get this clearly in mind!

"Birthright," as defined above, includes only that which comes by right of birth. No one can receive eternal life as a *right*, from natural birth. If it were our right, inherited by birth, it would not be by grace. Salvation comes by *grace*—God's *gift*, by undeserved pardon—unmerited favor. We can receive only *material* possessions as a right by

37

birth. And when that right is passed down through generations to ever-multiplying descendants, it finally devolves into a NATIONAL inheritance. It confers only material possessions, power, or position. It does *not* bestow *spiritual* blessings. It is a matter of race, not grace!

There is another distinction between a birthright and grace we ought to understand. A birthright, as before stated, is normally passed on from father to eldest son. There are no conditions which the recipient is required to meet. The son does nothing to qualify for it. He receives it as his right for no other reason than that he happened to be born his father's son. He has a right to it without earning it or qualifying to be worthy of it. He could, however, *disqualify* himself to keep, or even to receive it.

But the gift of immortality received by grace *does* have qualifying conditions! It is not your right, nor mine, to receive the gift of eternal life—to be actually *born* as God's son—literally a member of the God FAMILY! Think what conditions would result if it were! A rebellious, defiant, hostile, God-hating criminal or atheist could shake his fist at God and say: "Look, God! I hate you. I defy you! I refuse to obey you! But I *demand* your gift of eternal life! It's my RIGHT! I want to be born into your divine family—to receive all the vast POWER of a son of God, so I can use that power to oppose you! I want to make your family a house divided against itself. I will cause friction, hostility, hatred, unhappiness among all your children! I demand that POWER, as your *gift*, as my *right*, so that I may abuse that power—use it for EVIL!"

Grace Requires Conditions

Most professing "Christians"—and many teachings of what is called "traditional Christianity"—say there are no conditions, nothing that *we* must do to receive God's glorious grace. They deny that God requires obedience to His law! They twist the truth around by saying that would be *earning* one's salvation! They *do* demand it of God, while they still rebel against His law and refuse to keep it!

Think where that would lead! Understand this! Eternal life is, indeed, God's free gift. You can't earn it! But it is not your right! You cannot demand it of God as your right, while you defy God, rebel against His government, refuse to let Him rule your life His way!

Therefore God has imposed CONDITIONS! Those conditions do not earn you a thing! But God *gives* His Holy Spirit to those who obey Him (Acts 5:32). He does not pay it—but the passage speaks of the Holy Spirit which "God hath *given* to them *that obey Him*." It is still a free GIFT!

A rich man might have seven men standing before him, and say: "I will *give*, as my free GIFT, $1,000 to any or all of you who will step forward to receive it." Their stepping forward does not EARN it. It is merely the *condition* required to receive the free GIFT.

The word "grace" means unmerited, undeserved *pardon!* God *pardons* those who REPENT! And "repent" means to *turn from* rebellion, hostility, disobedience. "Repent" means to turn to obedience to God's law. The fact that God chooses *not* to give this wonderful gift— this gift of immortality, which carries with it divine power—to those who would misuse it for harm and evil; the fact that He chooses to give it only to those who will rightly use it—does not mean it comes by *works* instead of grace. If there were *no* conditions, then everyone could demand it—and it would be received as a right by birth, instead of by grace!

The very *fact* of grace makes necessary God's required qualifications. But it still is an undeserved GIFT!

Obedience does not earn anything—that is only what we *owe* to God. A birthright requires no qualification. It is a right by birth.

What the Birthright Conferred

Just what special material inheritance was passed on by the birthright few have understood. Yet it conferred the

"He must indeed have a blind soul who cannot see that some great purpose and design is being worked out here below."

(Winston Churchill)

richest, most valuable material inheritance ever passed from father to son—the most colossal wealth and power ever amassed by man or empire! The magnitude of this birthright is staggering!

It includes all the first phase of God's tremendous promises to Abraham. This legacy guaranteed on the authority of God Almighty, *unconditionally*, multitudinous population, untold wealth and material resources, national greatness and world power!

Not only had God promised that a world-dominant

nation and a company, or commonwealth, of nations whose peoples descended from Abraham would be as populous as the grains of sand of the seashore—as the stars in multitude; not only did He promise they should possess the *gate* (Fenton translation: gates) of enemy nations, which alone signifies world dominance and power; but the birthright finally included vast material wealth and unlimited national resources. That was made plain in the blessing given to Jacob, as we shall soon see.

The Birthright Denied to Ishmael

Except in cases of divine intervention, which occurred three times, the inheritance of the birthright fell automatically to the eldest son in each generation.

Isaac was chosen by the Eternal to inherit both the sceptre and birthright. Abraham had other sons. Ishmael was the eldest. But God chose Isaac, and "Abraham gave all that he had unto Isaac" (Gen 25:5). Isaac, however, was Abraham's firstborn *lawful* son. Ishmael was the son of Hagar, Sarah's Egyptian handmaid.

Abraham loved Ishmael and desired for him to have the birthright. "And Abraham said unto God, O that Ishmael might live before thee!" (Gen. 17:18.)

Sarah his wife was barren. "And God said, Sarah thy wife shall bear thee a son indeed; and thou shalt call his name Isaac: and I will establish my covenant with him for an everlasting covenant, and with his seed after him. And as for Ishmael, I . . . will make him fruitful, and will multiply him exceedingly . . . and I will make him a great nation. But my covenant will I establish with Isaac . . ." (verses 19-21).

Regarding the future nation to spring from Ishmael, the angel of the Eternal had said to Hagar: "He

41

will be a wild man; his hand will be against every man, and every man's hand against him; and he shall dwell to the east [correct translation] of all his brethren" (Gen. 16:12).

Two clues are given here: 1) Ishmael's descendants were to become a great nation but the birthright nations were to be greater; and 2) they were to dwell to the east of their brethren—that is, of Isaac's descendants who had the birthright. The children of Ishmael have become the Arabs of today. The nation and company of nations who hold the birthright must, therefore, be larger, wealthier, more powerful, and must be found geographically west of the Arab nations.

Abraham was the human type of God the Father, and Isaac of Christ. There are many parallels. Space prohibits expounding them here, except to note that if we are Christ's we are Abraham's children (Gal. 3:29), and Abraham is the "*father* of the faithful" (see Gal. 3:7); that Abraham was called on to be willing to sacrifice his only (legitimate) son (Gen. 22:2) even as God gave His only begotten Son, Jesus Christ, for the sins of the world; that Isaac's wife Rebekah is a type of the Church, and she had to fall in love with him and accept him as her husband before she saw him with her eyes; and that Isaac was born *by promise,* and by a miracle from God, even as Jesus was miraculously born of the virgin Mary.

Isaac had twin sons, Esau and Jacob. Esau was the firstborn, and therefore the legal inheritor of the birthright. But Esau undervalued it and sold it to Jacob.

Esau Sells the Birthright

God had chosen Jacob to possess these promises before the twins were born. But Jacob, influenced by his mother instead of waiting on the Eternal, resorted to deception and took it from Esau.

The Eternal had said to Rebekah, regarding Esau and Jacob, that they were the beginning of two nations—"two manner of people . . . the one people shall be stronger than the other people," said God, "and the elder shall serve the younger" (Gen. 25:23).

Their descendants, then, were to become two different types of people. The story of Jacob's premature and deceptive acquisition of the birthright continues, in Genesis 25:27-34.

"And the boys grew: and Esau was a cunning hunter, a man of the field; and Jacob was a plain man, dwelling in tents. And Isaac loved Esau, because he did eat of his venison: but Rebekah loved Jacob. And Jacob sod pottage [boiled porridge—Fenton's translation]: and Esau came from the field, and he was faint: And Esau said to Jacob, Feed me, I pray thee, with that same red pottage; for I am faint: therefore was his name called *Edom*."

"Edom" means, literally, "red soup," and is so translated in the Fenton version. It will prove another "key" to Bible understanding for the reader to carefully fasten in his memory the fact that "Edom" refers to ESAU. Many prophecies pertaining to the present and future employ the name Edom. They cannot be understood unless it is realized that they refer to the descendants of Esau, primarily the Turkish nation today.

"And Jacob said, Sell me this day thy birthright. And Esau said, Behold, I am at the point to die: and what profit shall this birthright do to me? And Jacob said, Swear to me this day; and he sware unto him: and he sold his birthright unto Jacob. Then Jacob gave Esau bread and pottage of lentiles; and he did

HUGE FLOCKS OF SHEEP *were among the blessings promised to Abraham's descendants.*

---

eat and drink, and rose up, and went his way: thus Esau despised his birthright." Later, Jacob subtly took from Esau his blessing. The story of this deception is found in Genesis 27.

Jacob's Deception

It was at a time when Isaac was old, his eyesight dimmed with age. Nearing the end of his life, he called Esau and requested that he go to the field and hunt for venison, prepare it and bring it to him. He would then bestow the blessing confirming the birthright.

But Rebekah overheard, and sent Jacob quickly for two kids of the goats. These she prepared in the same tempting way that Isaac loved his venison. Then she took some of Esau's clothes and put them on Jacob. Now Esau was very hairy, while Jacob was smooth, so Rebekah carefully placed the skins of the two kids upon Jacob's hands, arms, and smooth part of his neck.

In this disguise, with his imitation venison, Jacob went in to receive his father's blessing. "And Jacob said unto his father, I am Esau thy firstborn" (Gen. 27:19).

44

BLESSING: *golden wheat—millions of acres—promised to the birthright nations.*

Isaac was surprised he had found the venison so quickly and became suspicious. Jacob lied again, asserting the Eternal had brought the venison to him. Isaac detected the voice was that of Jacob.

"And Isaac said unto Jacob, Come near, I pray thee, that I may feel thee, my son, whether thou be my very son Esau or not. And Jacob went near unto Isaac his father; and he felt him, and said, The voice is Jacob's voice, but the hands are the hands of Esau. And he discerned him not, because his hands were hairy, as his brother Esau's hands: so he blessed him" (verses 21-23).

What the Birthright Included

Now notice carefully what that blessing included!

"And his father Isaac said unto him, Come near now, and kiss me, my son. And he came near, and kissed him: and he smelled the smell of his raiment, and blessed him, and said, See, the smell of my son is as the smell of a field which the Eternal hath blessed: Therefore God give thee of the dew of heaven, and the fatness of the earth, and plenty of corn and wine [Fenton's

45

translation: increase and possession]: Let people serve thee, and nations bow down to thee: be lord over thy brethren, and let thy mother's sons bow down to thee: cursed be every one that curseth thee, and blessed be he that blesseth thee" (verses 26-29).

Note it! Materialistic promises, *national* in nature, every one! Not one of them pertaining to salvation. None having to do with life after death. Nothing spiritual here! All pertaining purely to this present fleshly life! NATIONAL prosperity—rainfall, plenty of corn and wine, the fatness of the earth, or, as the margin reads, the fat places of the earth—increase and possession. "*Nations* shall bow down to thee!" "Let people serve thee."

When Esau returned and found how Jacob had supplanted him, he was very bitter. He pleaded for a blessing, too. But Isaac could not retract the blessing given to Jacob. So he passed on to Esau the following prophecy:

"Behold, thy dwelling shall be [correct translation: away from] the fatness of the earth, and of the dew of heaven from above; and by thy sword shalt thou live, and shalt serve thy brother; and it shall come to pass when thou shalt have the dominion, that thou shalt break his yoke from off thy neck. And Esau hated Jacob . . . " (verses 39-41).

In verse 39, quoted above, the Hebrew preposition *min* should be translated "from" or "away from," not "of." Actually, the prophesied lot of Esau was more of a curse than a blessing. The Revised Standard Version translates it: "Behold, away from the fatness of the earth shall your dwelling be, and away from the dew of heaven on high." Moffatt renders it: "Far from rich soil on earth shall you live, far from the dew of heaven on high." Actually, the Hebrew words convey the *dual* meaning, and *both* have happened to Esau's descendants.

Prophecy for Turkey

The sparse records of history, with other proofs, show that many of the descendants of Esau became known as Turks. Therefore we must remember that all prophecies pertaining to the latter days referring to Edom, or Esau, refer generally to the Turkish nation.

In Isaac's dying prophecy, he foretold that Esau's descendants would come to a time when they should have dominion, and then break the yoke of the Israelites from off their necks. That has happened. The children of Israel, through sin, were driven out of the promised land that belonged with the birthright. The Turks came to power and dominion and for many centuries possessed that land. Those descendants, the Turkish people, occupied Palestine 400 years before Britain took it in 1917. Esau's descendants always have lusted for that land, central promise of the birthright! The Turks have truly lived by the sword!

The Lesson for Us

But let's return to our story. Before Jacob was born, God had spoken to his mother and revealed to her that Jacob should receive the birthright. Instead, however, of waiting for the Eternal to bring this about in His own way, she schemed with Jacob to take it by lying and deception.

There is a lesson here for us today. As Isaac is, in a sense, a type of Christ, so Rebekah is, in a sense, a type of the Church, in which still dwells weakness and carnality.

Sometimes we become too much in a hurry. We ask the Almighty for things He has promised in His Word. Then we try to dictate to Him just *how* and *when* it shall be accomplished! We need to learn to "wait upon the Lord." He always does things in His way, and in His own time. And He distinctly tells us that His ways are not our ways! Once we commit a thing to the Almighty, let us have not only the trust, but the respect, for the One so great, that we will leave the matter in His hands.

Had Jacob trusted the Eternal instead of taking this into his own hands in a wrong way, the birthright would have come to him more honorably. Under the circumstances, Jacob, which name means "supplanter," had far more difficulty securing *God's* blessing upon the precious possession than his predecessors.

But after years of trial and test—after finally wrestling all night with the angel (Gen. 32:24-29)—after confessing his name as "supplanter"—God bestowed His blessing upon Jacob, took away his reproachful name, and gave him a new, untainted name, ISRAEL—which means "prevailer," or "overcomer with God."

And thus we see that through Abraham, Isaac, and Jacob, the promises were handed down to one man at a time. There was no branching out toward national growth until the days of Jacob. For three generations it had been a "one-man nation." But Jacob had twelve sons, and through them the future *great nation* and *company of nations* were started on their way.

Reuben Lost the Birthright

The next legal inheritor of the birthright was Reuben, firstborn son of Israel, by his first wife, Leah. But Reuben, like Esau, lost it. And Joseph, eleventh-born of Jacob, but firstborn of Rachel, his second and truly loved wife, received it.

The birthright belonged, legally, to Reuben, not Joseph. It is related in I Chronicles 5:1-2 how it fell to Joseph: "Now the sons of Reuben the firstborn of Israel, (for he was the firstborn; but, forasmuch as he defiled his father's bed, his birthright was given unto the sons of Joseph the son of Israel: and the genealogy is not to be reckoned after the birthright [or, RSV, "so that he (Reuben) is not enrolled in the genealogy according to the birthright"]. For *Judah* prevailed above his brethren, and of *him came to the chief ruler*; but the BIRTHRIGHT WAS JOSEPH'S)."

So at this point the two divisions of the Abrahamic promises—the birthright, involving material and national promises, and the sceptre, including the kingly and spiritual promises—were separated.

It is of first importance to keep in mind that the birthright, including the promised land now called Palestine, the assurance of multitudinous population, material and national prosperity, dominance over other nations, *was now given to* JOSEPH *and his sons.*

Mark that well! This BIRTHRIGHT was not to be inherited by *all* the tribes of Israel! It was not given to the Jews! Only a part of the Israelites—the *descendants of Joseph*—was to inherit these tremendous *national* promises!

These material promises for *this* life, then, belonged to an altogether different tribe among the children of Israel than the sceptre promise of the kingly line culminating in Jesus Christ, which spiritual promise belonged in the tribe of Judah!

These national promises of the multitudinous seed then became the possession of an altogether different *tribe* than the promise of the one seed, Christ, who sprang from Judah! This fact of the two sets of promises, stressed in the preceding chapter, ought to be plain and clear to every reader by now.

Fix it permanently in mind. It is one of the vital keys to Bible understanding!

49

At the time of Jacob's death, he and his sons were living in Egypt. We assume, of course, that you are familiar with the story of how Joseph was sold by his brothers into Egypt; of how he there became food administrator and prime minister, next under the king and in actual rule of the nation; of the seven years of plenty, followed by seven years of famine, in which food had been stored only in Egypt under Joseph's supervision; of the visit of Joseph's brothers to Egypt in quest of food, and how Joseph induced them to bring their father and brother Benjamin down to Egypt; and finally, of the dramatic revelation of Joseph's identity to his brethren, amid weeping and rejoicing.

And how prophetic that was! As we shall see, Joseph, in his descendants, shall soon once again have his true identity revealed to his brothers—and to the world. And how *hidden* from the world is that identity now!

Birthright to Joseph's Sons

And now the time came to pass on the birthright to another generation. Let us re-create the dramatic scene.

It occurred in Egypt, after Joseph had succeeded in having his father brought there, as well as all his brothers. Joseph, remember, was prime minister of the nation.

It was reported to Joseph that Jacob, his father, was ill. He took with him his two sons, Manasseh and Ephraim, sons of an Egyptian mother, and hastened to the dying patriarch's bedside.

"And Israel strengthened himself, and sat upon the bed. And Jacob said unto Joseph, God Almighty appeared unto me at Luz in the land of Canaan, and blessed me, and said unto me, Behold, I will make thee fruitful, and multiply thee, and I will make of thee a

50

"And Jacob went near unto Isaac his father; and he felt him, and said, The voice is Jacob's voice, but the hands are the hands of Esau."

(Genesis 27:22)

multitude of people; and will give this land to thy seed after thee for an everlasting possession" (Gen. 48:2-4).

Notice carefully these promises!

The birthright is about to be passed on to another generation. Notice that nothing whatsoever is said about *all* the families of the earth being blessed in his seed— the ONE seed. Nothing is said about kings. Nothing is said about spiritual blessings whatever. *These* promises are those of the birthright. *These* promises are of *multiple seed*—a multitude of people—and *possession of the promised land.* Now let us continue.

"And now thy two sons, Ephraim and Manasseh, which were born unto thee in the land of Egypt before I came unto thee into Egypt, are mine; as Reuben and Simeon, they shall be mine" (verse 5).

Thus did Jacob *adopt* Joseph's two sons, making

51

them, legally, his own sons. This, no doubt, was done because they were half-blooded Egyptians. Israel made them his own adopted sons, so the birthright could be passed on to them. Notice, too, that in the first verse of this 48th chapter of Genesis, Manasseh's name is mentioned first, because Manasseh was the elder. But old Jacob now mentioned the name of Ephraim first. Here we see supernatural guidance!

Jacob said to Joseph: "Bring them, I pray thee, unto me, and I will bless them. Now the eyes of Israel were dim for age, so that he could not see" (verses 9-10).

The birthright, remember, belongs legally to the firstborn, unless altered by divine intervention. The inheritor of the birthright, in receiving the blessing conferred upon him, should have had Jacob's *right* hand resting upon his head. That is why "Joseph took them both, *Ephraim* in his right hand *toward Israel's left hand*, and *Manasseh* in his left hand *toward Israel's right hand*, and brought them near unto him" (verse 13).

Name Israel Given to Joseph's Sons

But once again the Eternal intervened in conferring this momentous birthright! Jacob, though blind so he could not see the lads before him, *crossed his hands*, "and Israel stretched out his right hand, and laid it upon Ephraim's head, who was the younger, and his left hand upon Manasseh's head, guiding his hands wittingly; for Manasseh was the firstborn. And he blessed Joseph, and said, God, before whom my fathers Abraham and Isaac did walk, the God which fed me all my life long unto this day, the Angel which redeemed me from all evil, bless the lads; and *let my name be named on them*, and the name of my fathers Abraham and Isaac; and let them grow into a multitude in the midst of the earth" (verses 14-16).

Let *who* grow into this promised multitude? Let *whose* descendants become that numerous seed, which shall number into billions? Not Judah, the father of the Jews—note it!—but EPHRAIM AND MANASSEH! Why have the eyes and understanding of church leaders and Bible students been blinded to this plain fact of Scripture?

Notice, Israel did not confer this blessing on just one, but on *both*—"Bless the lads," he said. This blessing went upon them jointly. "Let my name be named on them" was part of this blessing. His name was ISRAEL. Hence, it was the descendants of *these* lads, not the descendants of Judah, or the Jews, who were named ISRAEL. How clear it is that the name ISRAEL was to be indelibly stamped on EPHRAIM and MANASSEH!

A shocking fact—and yet plainly *proved*, right before your eyes! And remember, this scripture needs no "interpretation" or "special meaning" or "hidden symbolism" for you to understand! Here is the plain, simple statement that Jacob's name, which was changed to *Israel*, would become the very POSSESSION and *property*—the label on the peoples of Ephraim and Manasseh!

WHO, then, according to your Bible, is the real Israel (racially and nationally) of today?

Ephraim and Manasseh!

Ephraim and Manasseh *together* received the *right* to the name ISRAEL. It was to become the national name of their descendants. And their descendants were never Jews! Fix this fact firmly in your mind!

Thus it is that many of the prophecies about "Israel" or "Jacob" do not refer to Jews or to any of the nations that are today the descendants of the other tribes of Israel. Mark that well! Few, indeed, are the clergymen, theologians, or professed Bible scholars who know that today. Many *refuse* to know it!

Together the descendants of these two lads, Ephraim and Manasseh, were to grow into the promised multitude—the nation and company of nations. These national blessings are poured upon them jointly. These are the collective blessings which the lads together received—but not the other tribes!

Jacob Crosses Hands

But at this juncture, Joseph noticed that Jacob's right hand was not resting upon the head of the firstborn. He endeavored to remove it.

"Not so, my father," said Joseph, "for this is the firstborn; put thy right hand upon his head. And his father refused, and said, I know it, my son, I know it: he [Manasseh] also shall become a people, and he also shall be great: but truly *his younger brother shall be greater than he*, and his seed shall become a multitude [or, COMPANY] of nations. And he blessed them that day, saying, In thee shall Israel bless, saying, God make thee as Ephraim and as Manasseh: and he set Ephraim before Manasseh" (Gen. 48:18-20). Here the promises are no longer collective, possessed jointly. Jacob now was prophesying as to the blessings of each, individually.

As we have seen from the preceding chapter, the numerous seed was to become "a nation, and a company of nations." Now we see that the "nation" to become truly great is to spring from the seed of Manasseh, the son of Joseph. The "company of nations" is to grow out of Ephraim. Notice that, before dividing the promises, this prophetic blessing indicated plainly that the descendants of these lads should remain *together*, and together grow into a great multitude, then become separated, Manasseh becoming a *great nation*, and Ephraim a still greater *company of nations*.

54

Here, then, is yet another detail of the future national characteristics of these people. We must not look for the fulfillment among the sons of Judah. Nor among descendants of any other of the twelve tribes.

The promise of a future great nation and a company of nations, together great for multitude, rich in national material prosperity, possessing the "gates" of the earth's other nations, applies solely to these lads and the two tribes which sprang from them.

We might add here, too, that the tribes of Ephraim and Manasseh never became such in the times of Bible history. Some might suppose the house of Judah was the nation, and the ten tribes, the company of nations. But *none* of these promises went to Judah. Nor were they to be fulfilled in any of the other tribes, save Joseph's double portion, the two tribes of Ephraim and Manasseh!

It was Ephraim who was to become the company, or multitude, of nations, and Manasseh who was to become the great single nation. And these promises never were fulfilled in them, in times of Bible history. If these promises ever have been fulfilled, we must look for their fulfillment between the close of Bible history and the present!

Prophecy for Today

While still in the spirit of prophecy, Jacob called his twelve sons together to tell them what their posterity should become *"in the last days."*

Here are prophecies which should assist us in identifying the tribes of Israel *today*—for surely these are the *last days*! We shall here take space to consider only the destiny of Judah and of Joseph. Joseph's descendants were actually divided into two tribes, Ephraim and Manasseh, and usually are called by those tribal names instead of the name "Joseph." The fact that these tribes are here spoken of as "Joseph" plainly indicates that the prophecy applies jointly to Ephraim and Manasseh.

"And Jacob called unto his sons, and said, Gather yourselves together, that I may tell you that which shall befall you *in the last days*. . . . Judah, thou art he whom thy brethren shall praise: thy hand shall be in the neck of thine enemies; thy father's children shall bow down before thee. Judah is a lion's whelp: from the prey, my son, thou art gone up: he stooped down, he couched as a lion, and as an old lion; who shall rouse him up? The sceptre shall not depart from Judah, nor a lawgiver [margin, ruler's staff] from between his feet, until Shiloh come; and unto him shall the gathering of the people be" (Gen. 49:1, 8-10). The Hebrew word here translated *Shiloh* means the Messiah, the Prince of Peace, or the one *"seed"* of Abraham. (See *Young's Analytical Concordance to the Holy Bible.*)

Promised to Joseph

Regarding Joseph, the combined Ephraim-Manasseh tribes, at this present day, Israel prophesied: "*Joseph is a fruitful bough* [here is pictured the birthright promise of multitudes in fulfillment], even a fruitful bough by a well; whose branches [margin, *daughters*] run over the wall" (verse 22).

In other words, in the last days we are to find the children of Joseph a numerous people, a great nation and a company of nations, whose daughters, or children, shall "run over the wall"—that is, run over, or past, the nation's boundary—in other words, be a colonizing people! Further, in the prophecy for Joseph for these "last days": " . . . the Almighty . . . shall bless thee with blessings of heaven above, blessings of the deep that lieth under, blessings of the breasts, and of the womb: the blessings of thy father have prevailed above the blessings of my progenitors unto the utmost bound of the everlasting hills: they shall be on the head of Joseph, and on the crown of the head of him that was separate from [margin: is prince among] his brethren" (verses 25-26).

We shall see that these descendants of Joseph, possessing these birthright promises—to become numerous, to colonize, thus spreading to the "north and the south, and east and the west," until they encircled the globe, to possess the "gates" of enemy nations—never returned to Jerusalem from Assyria, where they were driven with the ten tribes after 721 B.C., and were never again mixed with Jews from that time! Here are promises and prophecies which never have been fulfilled by the Jews, by the Church, by the American Indian, or any other fanciful counterparts of modern Israel. But they *are fulfilled* today if the Word of God is to stand!

5

The Davidic Covenant

AFTER THE DEATH OF JACOB AND
his twelve sons in Egypt, their children grew in about two and a quar-
ter centuries to a population probably between two and
three million in that land.

But Israel's children became slaves: "And Joseph
died, and all his brethren, and all that generation. And
the children of Israel were fruitful, and increased abun-
dantly, and multiplied, and waxed exceeding mighty;
and the land was filled with them. Now there arose up a
new king over Egypt, which knew not Joseph. . . . And
the Egyptians made the children of Israel to serve with
rigour: and they made their lives bitter with hard bondage . . ." (Ex. 1:6-14).

Then God raised up Moses and fitted him in a
special way to lead these children of Israel out of the
bondage that had come to them in Egypt.

When they reached Mt. Sinai, in the peninsula wilderness, God made a covenant with them establishing them as a NATION—*His* nation—among the kingdoms of the world. Their government was theocratic, with the civil, as well as the spiritual and religious laws, given directly from God. God Himself was their King and He ruled them by a system of judges.

Israel's First King Was God

God was Israel's only King! Israel was *both* church and state. In Acts 7:38 we are told that the Israelites formed the church in the wilderness. The word "congregation" of Israel used throughout the Old Testament has the same meaning exactly as the word "church" in the New. Israel, consequently, had more than one set of laws. God gave Israel a twofold form of government. The congregation, or church, was given ritualistic laws—animal sacrifices, meat and drink offerings, carnal or fleshly ordinances.

But Israel also was a *civil* government; thus for it God established civil officers and civil laws—statutes and judgments. The one great central code of law, basis for both church and civil government—the overall SPIRITUAL CODE—was the TEN COMMANDMENTS, spoken by God directly to all the congregation, written with the very finger of God in tables of stone.

For several generations after leaving Egypt, God was their King! (This history is found through the books of Moses, Joshua and Judges.) Each tribe kept separate by itself, but together they formed one nation in much the same manner as the United States is one nation composed of individual states.

Each tribe occupied its own land, or district. The Levites became the priestly tribe, mingling throughout the other tribes, having no inheritance in the land and no separate territory (except for cities) of their own. To offset this, however, the children of Joseph were divided into *two* tribes—Ephraim and Manasseh—thus leaving twelve distinct and separate tribes, each occupying its own territory or province, *in addition to* the Levites who were sprinkled among the tribes.

All these years the birthright and the sceptre remained within the one nation—the birthright, of course, being handed down through the tribes of Ephraim and Manasseh, the sceptre with Judah.

Dissatisfied With God

The children of Israel were human, even as you and I. They continually grumbled and complained. Their carnal minds were hostile to God and His laws, even as human minds today (Rom. 8:7). Soon they became dissatisfied with God as their King and demanded that a *man* should be their king as in the Gentile nations around them. So today, we want to be like the non-Christians around us instead of conforming strictly to the ways of God as we are instructed in His Word! Human nature has ever been thus.

When the elders of Israel came to Samuel demanding a man be made their king, it naturally displeased Samuel, their prophet. But the Eternal said: "Hearken unto the voice of the people in all that they say unto thee: for they have not rejected thee, *but they have rejected me, that I should not reign over them. . . .* howbeit yet protest solemnly unto them, and shew them the manner of the king that shall reign over them" (I Sam. 8:7-9).

Saul was their first human king. He refused obedience to God and was finally rejected. He was slain in battle. His sole surviving son, Ishbosheth, was slain after a reign of only two years (II Sam. 2:10). However, Ishbosheth never reigned over Judah. With this short reign over part of Israel, Saul's dynasty ceased. That is how God rejected him. His dynasty was cut off!

David's Dynasty Forever

David succeeded Saul. David sat on the *Eternal's throne*. David's son Solomon succeeded him, also sitting on the Eternal's throne. "Then Solomon sat on *the throne of the Eternal* as king instead of David his father" (I Chron. 29:23; see also II Chron. 9:8).

I wish here to impress another special point. Before Saul, the Eternal had been King over Israel. These human kings were sitting upon the Eternal's throne. The Eternal—"Lord"—is Jesus Christ who was with the Father before the world was (John 17:5 and 1:1-2,14). Jesus is both the "root" *and* the "offspring" of David (Rev. 22:16). Since He was the "root," the throne was His before David was born. David merely sat upon the Eternal's throne. Secondly, since Jesus was David's lawful fleshly Son, this same throne shall once more become His right by inheritance, continuing David's dynasty. And so, when Christ returns to earth, David's throne will be doubly His right!

Now we come to a seemingly incredible fact—fantastic—almost unbelievable, but *true!* While David was king, God made with him a perpetual covenant, unconditionally, which God cannot and will not break! This covenant is even more amazing, and less understood, than the unconditional covenant with Abraham!

I want you now to plant firmly in mind the specific nature and character of the covenant the Almighty made with David. For it is a vital link in the purpose and mission of Christ—an important KEY to Bible understanding!

In II Samuel 23:1, 5, we find: "Now these be the last

words of David. . . . God . . . hath made with me *an everlasting covenant,* ordered in all things, and *sure."* In other words, a covenant that shall endure forever and *cannot fail!*

Turn back to the seventh chapter of II Samuel for more specific details. God gave David this covenant promise at a time when David was much concerned over the Ark of the Covenant dwelling in a tent. David wanted to build a great temple at Jerusalem.

"And it came to pass that night, that the word of the Lord came unto Nathan, saying, Go and tell my servant David, Thus saith the Lord, Shalt thou build me an house for me to dwell in? . . . When thy days be fulfilled, and thou shalt sleep with thy fathers, I will set up thy seed after thee, which shall proceed out of thy bowels [Solomon], and I will establish his kingdom. He shall build an house for my name, *and I will stablish the throne of his kingdom for ever.* I will be his father, and he shall be my son. If he commit iniquity, I will chasten him with the rod of men, and with the stripes of the children of men: But my mercy shall not depart away from him, as I took it from Saul, whom I put away before thee. *And thine house and thy kingdom shall be established for ever* before thee: THY THRONE SHALL BE ESTABLISHED FOR EVER" (II Sam. 7:4-5, 12-16).

Points to Notice

Notice carefully these points:

1) David's throne was set up and established with Solomon, David's son.

2) The throne—David's throne (verse 16)—was established FOREVER in Solomon (verse 13). Observe that this nowhere says that when Christ comes, God will establish it in *Him* forever. It says it was to be established forever *in Solomon.*

3) What if Solomon, or the children of Israel, disobey? Would that cancel this covenant? Verses 14-15 plainly say that if they commit iniquity, God will chasten them *with the rod of men,* but will NOT break this covenant. The throne shall go on forever just the same!

4) Notice particularly, in case of disobedience, God will *not* take the throne away as He took it from Saul. How did He take it from Saul? Saul's dynasty ended! No son of Saul ever sat on the throne. But Solomon's dynasty would not end. The punishment for disobedience would be chastening at the hands of *men.*

5) Since God did firmly establish this throne with David and with Solomon, if David's throne ceased from existence, even for the length of one generation, could we say it had been established *forever* as God here promised?

Here is the fact as little realized as any in the Bible! Almighty God made an absolutely binding—just *how* binding we shall see!—covenant with David, *unconditionally* guaranteeing that there should never be a single generation from that time forward when there would not be a descendant of David, in UNBROKEN DYNASTY sitting on David's throne, ruling over children of Israel! It was the promise of a continuous, unbroken dynasty—all generations *forever*—that was guaranteed.

This is hard to believe! Yet God promised and *unalterably guaranteed* just that! There were no conditions. Nothing that would happen could prevent it. The sins of the people were not to change it. The promise stood immutable!

The End of the Record

But where is that throne today?

The history of the Bible records a line of kings, all

63

Solomon sat on the Eternal's throne. God promised that Solomon's dynasty would never end; it would be continuous and unbroken through all generations forever.

(II Sam. 7:12-16)

descendants of David in continuous dynasty, down to King Zedekiah. But in the year 585 B.C. this last recorded king ever to sit on this throne was captured by the armies of King Nebuchadnezzar of Babylon, his eyes were put out, he was taken to Babylon, and there died in a dungeon!

Moreover, all his sons were slain! All the nobles of Judah who were not already imprisoned or enslaved at Babylon at that time were killed, so that none could remain to sit on the throne of David! The Chaldeans destroyed Jerusalem, burned the Temple and the king's houses, took the Jews, a captive, slave people to Babylon. There is certainly no record of any king of the line of David ruling over Judah from that day to this. However, the line of Jehoiakin to Jesus survived in Babylonish captivity—so Jesus was a descendant of David.

Some will say, however, that this throne is established today in Christ. But Christ has not yet taken over this throne! He pictured Himself as the nobleman (Luke 19:12) who went to a far country (heaven) to get for Himself a Kingdom, and, who, after receiving the right to the Kingdom, *would return.* Jesus Christ will not sit upon the throne of David until His second coming to earth, yet in the future!

But what of the nearly 600 years between King Zedekiah and the birth of Christ? *Who* was reigning over the Israelites and sitting on David's throne during those generations? If no one, then we must conclude God broke His Word, or the Scripture has been broken!

The answer is a mystery more astounding than any tale of fiction! The Bible reveals it, step by step.

But, then again, some will point to the expression "I *will* stablish" (II Sam. 7:13) and conclude that possibly God meant *at the second coming of Christ* He would establish that throne forever. And still that will not do. From whom would Christ take over David's throne if that throne has ceased these centuries to exist? But God plainly promised He would establish that throne *in Solomon:* "And I will stablish the throne of *his* [Solomon's] kingdom FOR EVER." He was not speaking of establishing it many centuries later in Christ—at His second coming. The "he" referred to is Solomon—not Christ, for God said: "If he commit iniquity, I will chasten him" (II Sam. 7:14).

But now I give you a scripture that ends all speculation as to *when* this throne was established: "Hear me, thou Jeroboam, and all Israel; ought ye not to KNOW that the Eternal God of Israel GAVE the kingdom over to Israel to David FOR EVER, even to him and to *his sons* by a covenant of salt?" (II Chron. 13:4-5.) The margin says "PERPETUAL covenant." This shows the establishing of the throne was then *in the past!* God gave, did give, this kingdom to David and his *sons*—not his *Son*, Christ, but his sons, plural—continuously forever.

Established for All Generations

"I have made a covenant with my chosen, I have sworn unto David my servant, Thy seed [dynasty—Moffatt] will I establish for ever, and build up *thy throne to all generations*" (Ps. 89:3-4). Note it! This throne, established forever, was built up to *all generations*. God *did* establish that throne, beginning with David and Solomon. We have a record of it for a number of generations—as far as King Zedekiah, 585 B.C.

It was established to *all* generations, continuously, perpetually, FOREVER! That term "all generations" certainly must include those generations from Zedekiah to the birth of Christ. Who occupied that throne during those generations?

Christ is not sitting on that throne now, but on the throne of Almighty God in heaven (Rev. 3:21).

So what about *this present generation?* Where is there a descendant of David today sitting in an unbroken line of kings on the throne of David, ruling over *children of Israel?*

Can one wonder that men like Thomas Paine and Robert Ingersoll lost faith in the Bible? They saw these unconditional promises, but they could not see how they had been kept. Yet, if we have patience, we shall see!

But to continue, in the 89th Psalm, with the 28th verse: "My mercy will I keep for him for evermore, and

66

my covenant shall stand fast with him. His seed [dynasty—Moffatt] also will I make to endure for ever, and *his throne as the days of heaven."*

Consider a moment the meaning of the word "seed" in this sense. Moffatt's translation in modern English properly translates it "dynasty." The Revised Standard Version translates it "his [David's] *line"*—that is, continuous line or succession of sons, generation after generation. This "seed" is not the general population of the children of Israel. This is speaking of David's seed, or David's sons. His sons were to be *kings.* David was of the tribe of Judah, possessor of the sceptre, not the birthright, promise. His "seed," therefore, was the *kingly* line. So, literally, it means his *dynasty,* his *line* of successive sons.

Now while his throne is enduring through all generations, as the days of heaven, consider the next verse: "If his children forsake my law, and walk not in my judgments; if they break my statutes, and keep not my commandments; then will I visit their transgression with the rod, and their iniquity with stripes. Nevertheless my lovingkindness will I not utterly take from him, nor suffer my faithfulness to fail. *My covenant will I not break,* nor alter the thing that is gone out of my lips. Once have I sworn by my holiness that I will not lie unto David. HIS SEED [dynasty] shall endure FOR EVER, and *his throne as the sun* before me. It shall be established for ever as the moon, and as a faithful witness in heaven" (Ps. 89:30-37).

This is speaking of those generations when his children may disobey and forsake God's law. Some today are excusing their inability to locate this throne by saying the covenant was *conditional*—that because the children of Israel disobeyed God, the covenant was broken. But what does the Almighty say? If the children disobey and transgress, they shall be *punished* for their

67

transgression—but *not* by the breaking of God's unconditional covenant with David!

Some say Christ took over the throne. But He didn't. Instead He was crucified, resurrected, and ascended to heaven. He *shall* come, and soon now, to sit upon that throne as the King of kings and Lord of lords. But how could Jesus Christ, when He returns again to earth, take over and sit upon a throne that long ago ceased to exist?

Will Christ Come to a Nonexistent Throne?

If the throne of David ceased with Zedekiah, then it does not exist today. And if it does not exist, *how shall Christ sit upon a nonexistent throne?* (See Luke 1:31-32.) And, since it was to continue through *all* generations, how about those many generations between Zedekiah and the birth of Jesus?

The very important *fact* that the glorified King of kings is coming to sit on an *existing throne* is further affirmed by the prophet Jeremiah. In the 33rd chapter is a prophecy of events to occur at the time of Christ's coming in supreme power and glory! At the time of writing this prophecy, the prophet was imprisoned in Jerusalem. The armies from Babylon were taking the Jews captive. God said to Jeremiah, "I will . . . shew thee great and mighty things, which thou knowest not. . . . concerning the houses of this city, and concerning the houses of the kings of Judah, which are thrown down . . ." (verses 3-4).

Jeremiah knew the kings' houses in Jerusalem were being destroyed—the throne of David *removed* from Jerusalem. He was, as will be shown later, to be God's agent in rooting out that throne from Jerusalem. God was now revealing to him a reassuring fact. The throne of David would, in this end time, be again planted in

Jerusalem. God now reassures the prophet that the throne will rule continuously over Israelites *until* that time. It will be the *same continuous* dynasty. The Messiah will sit on an existing throne!

Here is the prophecy of what is to happen at Christ's glorious coming to rule: "Behold, the days come, saith the Eternal, that I will perform that good thing which I have promised unto the house of Israel and to the house of Judah" (verse 14). Notice carefully! This *promise* of David's continuous dynasty is a promise to the *house of Israel*, as well as to Judah. Since the division into two nations, that throne had not been connected with Israel— only with Judah. But the promise to be fulfilled at Christ's coming connects it with Israel as well as Judah!

Continue: "In those days, and at that time, will I cause the Branch of righteousness [the Messiah] to grow up unto David; and he shall execute judgment and righteousness in the land" (verse 15). This speaks of Christ's rule as King of kings. Jesus, a descendant of David by human birth (Rom. 1:3), was the righteous *Branch*, or offshoot of David.

Continue: "In those days shall Judah be saved, and Jerusalem shall dwell safely. . . . For thus saith the Eternal; David shall never want a man to sit upon the throne of the house of Israel" (verses 16-17). Note it! It does not say David shall not, *finally*, after 2,500 years without a man on the throne, want for one. It says David shall NEVER—at any time—through all generations—want for a descendant to remain sitting on his throne!

And *over whom?*

Throne Not Over Jews

Not Judah! Read it in your own Bible! During these more than 2,500 years, David shall not want for a man to sit upon the throne of *the house of Israel*—not Judah!

The throne was, at the time God revealed this prophecy to Jeremiah, being rooted out of Judah. During these 2,500 years between then and Christ's coming, it was to be the throne of the house of ISRAEL!

After the coming of Christ to rule, it is evident that Israel is again to offer sacrifices, burnt offerings and meat offerings. In Ezekiel's prophecy, from the 40th chapter to the end of the book, covering this period after Christ's coming, these sacrifices are mentioned. But, after Christ's return, when they are again to be offered, the tribe of Levi will not have been destroyed—descendants of the priestly tribe will still be living. Notice verse 18 of Jeremiah 33: "Neither shall the priests the Levites want a man before me to offer burnt offerings, and to kindle meat offerings, and to do sacrifice continually."

This does *not* say they shall have, all these years prior to Christ's coming, continually offered sacrifices. Other scriptures show plainly sacrifices should *not* have been offered by Christians after Christ's own sacrifice, and they *were* not offered by Jews after the destruction of the Temple in A.D. 70. But other prophecies already quoted show just as plainly that David's descendants should be ruling on David's throne through all generations, beginning with Solomon.

Since many of the Levites undoubtedly remained among the Ten Tribes—although we know many continued among the Jews—and since those remaining among the Ten Tribes have *lost their identity* along with all Ten Tribes, it is entirely possible that many if not most, of the called true ministry of Jesus Christ through the centuries have been of the tribe of Levi.

Notice, now, how *binding* is God's covenant with David. "Thus saith the Eternal; If ye can break my covenant of the day, and my covenant of the night, and that there should not be day and night in their season; then may also my covenant be broken with David my servant, that he should not have a son to reign upon his throne . . ." (verses 20-21).

What People Say

Continue: "Considerest thou not what this people have spoken, saying, The two families which the Eternal hath chosen, he hath even cast them off? Thus they have despised my people, that they should be no more a nation before them" (verse 24).

That is what the *people* have been saying, as they were prophesied to say! They say the Jews were scattered among many, if not all, nations—scattered *individuals*—but no longer a nation having its own government! And the Ten Tribes were supposed to have been "lost," or to have gone out of existence, or to be just part of the scattered individual Jews! Yes, so the Jews themselves have said—and so the world has said! But what does GOD say?

Continue, next verse: "Thus saith the Eternal; If my covenant be not with day and night, and if I have not appointed the ordinances of heaven and earth; then will I cast away the seed of Jacob, and David my servant, so that I will not take any of his seed [dynasty] to be rulers over the seed of Abraham, Isaac, and Jacob: for I will cause their captivity to return, and have mercy on them" (verses 25-26).

The Test of Bible Truth

Strong words, those! Unless you can stop this old earth from turning on its axis—unless you can remove the sun and the moon and stars from heaven, says the Almighty, you cannot prevent Him from keeping His covenant to maintain *continuously, through all generations*, FOREV-

ER, from the time of David and Solomon, a descendant of David in one continuous dynasty on that throne!

He would not necessarily rule over *all* the house of Israel, or the Jews—but at least some of them, and enough to form a nation.

This *cannot* be applied to mean that there would not have been a continuous throne, or that it applies only to the "one seed"—Christ—finally coming to rule. Notice, it says specifically, ". . . so that I will not take any of his seed to be RULERS [more than one] over" Israelites. It is speaking of continuous, multiple rulers— not one Ruler coming to sit on a throne that 2,500 years before had ceased to exist!

The COVENANT PROMISE to David is plain and definite. Either his dynasty has continued and exists today, ruling over the house of ISRAEL (not the Jews), or God's Word fails!

Remember again the sceptre promise, which includes this line of kings until it culminates in CHRIST at His second coming: "The sceptre *shall not depart from Judah, nor a lawgiver* [margin, ruler's staff] *from between his feet, UNTIL* SHILOH [Christ] COME; and unto him shall the gathering of the people be" (Gen. 49:10).

Has the sceptre departed from Judah? *Has* the throne ceased? Or does it, as God so bindingly promised, exist today so that Christ can take over and sit upon a functioning, continuous throne when He comes?

The infallibility of the Bible is at stake! God's Word is at stake!

6

Children Of Israel Become Two Nations

THE HOUSE OF ISRAEL *is not Jewish!* Those who constitute it *are not Jews,* and never were! That fact we shall now see conclusively, beyond refute.

After David's death, his son Solomon succeeded him to the throne over Israel. Solomon taxed the people excessively and reigned in a gorgeous splendor probably never equalled before or since.

He also married Gentile wives from outside nations. Because of them, he burned incense and sacrificed to Moloch and other idols. As a result of this, "the Eternal said unto Solomon, Forasmuch as this is done of thee, and thou hast *not* kept my covenant and my statutes, which I have commanded thee, I will surely rend *the kingdom* from thee, and will give *it* to thy servant. Notwithstanding in thy days I will not do it for David thy father's sake: but I will rend it out of the hand of thy son. Howbeit I will not rend away ALL *the kingdom*; but will give *one tribe* to thy son for David my servant's sake, and for Jerusalem's sake which I have chosen" (I Kings 11:11-13).

Israel Separated from David's Throne

Note it! It is *the kingdom*, not part of it, which is to be rent away. It is the *part*, one tribe, which is to remain. And note—for right here is expressed the great WHY of this whole question—though Solomon himself deserved to have it rent away, God will leave one tribe, not because of leniency toward Solomon, but "FOR DAVID'S SAKE"!

God has made a perpetual covenant with David, unconditionally, which He cannot and will not break. David's dynasty cannot be broken! That is the reason the sceptre promise is not destroyed, but the ruler is to be permitted to rule on, without a single generation's gap, over at least a part of the children of Israel.

In I Kings 11:26 you read of Jeroboam, the son of Nebat, an Ephrathite, or Ephraimite, Solomon's servant. He was made ruler over the "house of Joseph"—or Ephraim and Manasseh.

Speaking to Jeroboam through Ahijah the prophet, the Eternal says: "Behold, I will rend the kingdom out of the hand of Solomon, and will give *ten tribes* to thee. . . . Howbeit I will not take the whole kingdom out of his hand . . . *for David my servant's sake,* whom I chose, *because* HE *kept my commandments and my statutes.* But I will take THE KINGDOM out of his son's hand, and will give it unto thee, even ten tribes. And unto his son will I give one tribe, *that David my servant* [remember *why*] may have a light alway before me in Jerusalem, the city which I have chosen me to put my name there. And I will take thee, and thou shalt reign according to all that

74

thy soul desireth, and shalt be *king over Israel"* (I Kings 11:31-37).

These words make plain two facts: The *nation* Israel is to be taken away from Solomon's son and given to Jeroboam. It is not just a tribe, or a few tribes, but *the nation* called by the title *Israel* which this Jeroboam, of the tribe of Ephraim, is to rule.

The ten-tribed kingdom was the one to which the national title "Israel" was given. For truly, the name "Israel" was named on the sons of Joseph! (Gen. 48:16.) Wherever *they* are, the Bible calls them by the national name ISRAEL. To the world, their identity today is lost. But, in biblical prophecy, it is *they*—not the Jews—who are called ISRAEL! And they were in, and headed, the ten-tribed nation ISRAEL.

On the other hand, because of His promise to David, the Eternal left one tribe, Judah, in Jerusalem under the sons of Solomon, so that a son of David might continue to sit on the throne of David over children of Israel. God had promised David, unconditionally, that the time would never come when he would not have a son or descendant sitting on the throne ruling over children of Israel.

Now, in later actual history, we see that promise being carried out—that covenant made *binding*! The children of Judah, though they do not constitute *all* the children of Israel and though they are not called by that national title, nevertheless *are* children of Israel, and thus God can keep His promise to David; can avoid abolishing the sceptre promises made to Abraham, Isaac and Jacob. And at the same time God can visit punishment upon Solomon by taking away the NATION Israel and leaving a son of the sceptre promise sitting on the throne over only one tribe. Note the very important point that, though a punishment must be inflicted, *God does not break any of His promises.*

David's Dynasty Rules Over Judah

God had promised that "the sceptre SHALL NOT DEPART FROM JUDAH." He did not break that promise. Now note carefully that the ten tribes, rent away, are called by the title "Israel," and that the one tribe remaining under Rehoboam, Solomon's son, is merely called "Judah" or the "house of Judah." They go by their tribal name, while the ten-tribed kingdom continues to carry the national name "Israel."

Actually, Israel rejected its king and set a *new* king, Jeroboam, on Israel's throne. The tribe of Judah *seceded* from the nation Israel in order to retain Rehoboam as *their* king. But now Rehoboam, David's grandson, became king of a *new* nation. That new nation was *not* the kingdom of Israel. It was the kingdom of *Judah!* Now see how it happened.

When Solomon's son, Rehoboam, succeeded to the throne, the people at once demanded that the heavy taxes imposed by Solomon be reduced. They sent their leader, Jeroboam, as spokesman, to Rehoboam.

Pleaded Jeroboam: "Thy father made our yoke grievous: now therefore make thou the grievous service of thy father, and his heavy yoke which he put upon us, lighter, and we will serve thee" (I Kings 12:4).

The reply was: "My father hath chastised you with whips, but I will chastise you with scorpions" (verse 11).

Israel rebelled. The command to the people was: "To your tents, O Israel"! The challenge to the royal family was: "Now see to thine own house"! (Verse 16.)

"So Israel rebelled against the house of David unto this day [the day this was written]. And it came to pass,

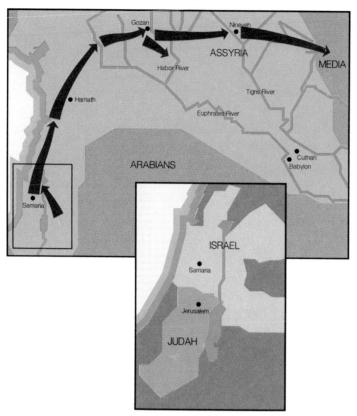

THE LARGE MAP ABOVE shows the various locations to which the ten tribes of Israel were carried captive by Assyria. Smaller map (inset) distinguishes the separate kingdoms of Judah and Israel.

---

when *all Israel* heard that Jeroboam was come again, that they sent and called him unto the congregation, and *made him king over* ALL ISRAEL: there was none that followed the house of David, *but the tribe of* JUDAH *only"* (I Kings 12:19-20).

Then "Rehoboam ... assembled all the HOUSE OF JUDAH, *with the tribe of Benjamin"* (verse 21). Rehoboam commenced to fight to subdue and bring back the house of Israel, but God said, "Ye shall not ... fight against your brethren the *children of Israel* . . . for this thing is from me" (verse 24).

Israel Divided into Two Nations

Did you notice that it is now the ten-tribed kingdom (headed by the Ephraim-Manasseh tribes with an Ephraimite as their king), the inheritor of the birthright promises, which is called the HOUSE OF ISRAEL?

The tribe of Judah left to Rehoboam, along with the Benjamites and later, after Jeroboam kicked them out of office in Israel, the priestly tribe of Levi, is called in Scripture, *not* Israel, but *the house of Judah.* They are all actually children of Israel but are no longer called by that national title. This is emphasized so much because the common conception is exactly the opposite.

The average conception today seems to be that the tribe of Judah which remained carried the title "Israel." Most people seem to think of the Ten Tribes as merely certain tribes driven out *from* the nation Israel.

But it is ISRAEL which now sets up its kingdom under the Ephraimite Jeroboam, in the land of Samaria, north of Jerusalem. It is not Israel, but *Judah*—a mere three tribes broken off from Israel—which is left behind in Jerusalem.

The Ten Tribes were not broken off from Israel. Israel did not remain in Jerusalem. Instead, *Judah was broken off from Israel.*

Israel at War with the Jews

Notice it carefully! The house of Judah, now including the tribe of Benjamin under King Rehoboam of David's dynasty, was about to fight against the nation Israel— with its ten tribes headed by Ephraim and Manasseh.

Now let us have scriptural *proof* that the ten-tribed

people called Israel, often prophetically spoken of as Ephraim, are not Jews and *never were Jews!* Remember that the term "Jew" is merely a nickname for "Judah." Hence, it applies to the one nation, or house of Judah *only*—never to the house of Israel.

From any exhaustive concordance you can learn that the first time in all the Bible that the word "Jew" occurs is in II Kings 16:6. Nowhere in all the Bible before this does the name "Jew" appear. Notice it!

Ahaz began to reign as king of Judah (verse 1). He sat on David's throne (verse 2). At this time, a man named Pekah was king of Israel. King Pekah of Israel formed an alliance with Rezin, king of Syria, *against* Judah, and together the armies of *Israel* and Syria, allied, came up against Jerusalem. They besieged King Ahaz of Judah, but could not overcome him (verse 5). "At that time," says verse 6, "Rezin king of Syria [the ally of Israel, fighting with Israel against Judah] recovered Elath to Syria, and drove the JEWS from Elath" (verse 6). The first place in the Bible where the word "Jew" is used, we find *Israel at war against the Jews!*

Who drove the *Jews* out of Elath? The *ally* of King Pekah of Israel! The army fighting *with* Israel *against* Judah. And the children of Judah who resided in the town of Elath are called Jews in a manner which distinguished them from the house of Israel, with whom these Jews were at war! Observe the significance of that!

The first place in Scripture where the name Jew appears, the *Jews were at* WAR *against* ISRAEL! They are of a different nation altogether. They are, individually, children of Israel. But they do not have that *national* title—house of Israel.

It is wrong to call the Jews of today "Israel." They are not the nation Israel—they are *Judah*! And wherever Israel is today, remember that Israel as a *national*

79

JERUSALEM (right) and Samaria (left) were the capital cities of the two separate nations Judah and Israel.

name *does not mean* JEW! Whoever the Lost Ten Tribes of Israel are today, *they are not the Jews!* Wherever you see the name "Israel," or "house of Israel," or "Samaria," or "Ephraim" used in prophecy, remember this: IT NEVER REFERS TO THE JEWS, but to Israel, which was at war against the Jews!

House of Israel Not Jews

No place in all the Bible does the term "Israel" refer to the Jews exclusively. When the sense is not national but individual, the term "Israel" alone, or "children of Israel," or "men of Israel" may, and sometimes does refer to or *include* the Jews. Such an expression, for instance, as "ye men of Israel," which frequently occurs in the New Testament, refers to Israelites as individuals in a collective sense, *not* a national sense. It usually refers to Jews as individual descendants of the patriarch Israel (Jacob).

Moses may not, scripturally, be called a Jew. He was a Levite. Abraham was not a Jew. Neither was Isaac nor Jacob—nor Adam or Noah for that matter. The descendants of the patriarch Judah are racially Jews and also all who joined themselves nationally to the

80

tribe of Judah—those of the tribes of Benjamin and Levi.

Jews are Israelites, just as Californians are Americans. But *most* Israelites are not Jews, just as most Americans are not Californians. The Jews are the house of Judah *only*, A PART of the Israelites. But when these people are spoken of as *nations*, rather than as collective individuals, the term "Israel" never refers to the Jews. "House of Israel" *never* means "Jews." The three tribes at Jerusalem under the Davidic king are called, merely, the *house of Judah.*

But of Ephraim and Manasseh, sons of Joseph, the dying Israel had said, "Let my name be named on *them*" (Gen. 48:16). And truly they now bear the name of Israel.

From here on, the tribe of Judah, with Benjamin and the tribe of Levi, is called "JUDAH"—*not* ISRAEL. The ten tribes, headed by Ephraim and Manasseh, from this time on are called "Israel." They are not Jews and never were called Jews! From this time on, the children of Israel, twelve tribes in all, are *divided into two nations!*

And now, for the first time, the birthright goes into one nation, Israel, headed by Ephraim-Manasseh, while the sceptre remains in *another nation*, called the "house of Judah." The two phases of the promises to Abraham now are divided between two entirely separate nations!

For many generations Israel and Judah remained as separate nations, in adjoining territories, having their own separate kings. Why should ministers and professed Bible students be in ignorance of this, when four whole books of the Bible, I and II Kings and I and II Chronicles, are devoted to explaining it and recording the history of these separate, rival kingdoms? Look at the maps in the back of your Bible. There you will see the territory of each nation plainly shown.

Judah retained the city of Jerusalem, its capital, and the territory known as Judea. Israel occupied the territory *north* of Judea. Samaria became its capital city, and the house of Israel often is called "Samaria" in prophecy. This, too, is a vital "key" to understanding prophecy. "Samaria" never refers to the Jews in prophecy—but always the *ten* tribes, the house of Israel.

We want to impress, here, that Israel and Judah are not two names for the same nation. They were, *and still are,* and shall be till the second coming of Christ, TWO SEPARATE NATIONS. The "house of Judah" *always* means "Jew." This distinction is vital, if we are to understand prophecy. Because most so-called Bible students are in ignorance of this basic distinction, they are unable to rightly understand prophecy!

The next place where the term "Jew" is mentioned in the Bible, the house of Israel had been driven out into captivity, lost from view, and the term applies *only* to those of the house of Judah.

Israel Rejects God's Rule

Immediately on becoming king over the house of Israel, Jeroboam (tribe of Ephraim) set up two golden calves, introducing idol worship in the kingdom (I Kings 12:28-33). Jeroboam was afraid lest his subjects, in going once a year to Jerusalem to keep the Feast of Tabernacles, should return to Rehoboam and he should lose his new throne. The introduction of idolatry was to prevent this and to keep the people home.

This idolatry with Sabbath-breaking (Ezek. 20:10-24) was the great national sin which became such a curse to Israel. Generation after generation God pleaded with the house of Israel to turn from tradition—from their

82

fathers' ways—and to return to keeping God's commandments. But through nine different dynasties under 19 kings, Israel continued these national sins—sins so great in God's sight that finally God caused them to become a conquered, captive nation.

Now let us note a passage which has been consistently misinterpreted. In I Kings 14:15-16 we find: "The Eternal shall smite Israel [not Judah], as a reed is shaken in the water, and he shall root up Israel out of this good land, which he gave to their fathers, and shall scatter them [not Judah] beyond the river, because they have made their groves, provoking the Eternal to anger. And he shall give Israel [not Judah] up because of the sins of Jeroboam, who did sin, and who made Israel to sin."

This is dealing specifically with the result of Jeroboam's idol worship in *Israel*—in the northern ten-tribed kingdom which possessed the birthright promises. It is *these* people who were to be rooted up and scattered beyond the river. Not the Jews. Yet this passage is quoted by nearly all students of prophecy as pertaining to the scattered condition of the Jews today—the very people to whom it does *not* apply. This is one example of the fact that what we are here covering is a veritable KEY to an understanding of many long-hidden prophecies. Unless this is kept firmly in mind, prophecy can never be correctly understood.

The people which this passage says shall be rooted up and scattered beyond the river never were called Jews. They were the people headed by Ephraim and Manasseh, possessors of the unconditional promises of becoming a great nation and a company of nations— becoming so numerous they would number into the hundreds of millions, possessing the gates of enemy nations, becoming a colonizing people, spreading out till their colonies spread around the globe.

Yet many who come to see this distinction between Israel and Judah—between Jews and the other tribes—after having seen it as a great new light, will, by force of years of habit, fall right back into the old rut and apply texts referring to Israel to the Jews!

The terms "house of Israel" or "all Israel," when the meaning is national, or the terms "Jacob," or "Rachel," or "Ephraim," or "house of Joseph," or "Samaria," often used in the Bible in prophecy, RELATE TO THE TEN-TRIBED BIRTHRIGHT PEOPLE, NOT TO THE JEWS. This is a KEY, and a master key, to Bible understanding!

Israel Driven Out and Lost

In the years 721-718 B.C., the house of Israel was conquered and its people were soon driven out of their own land—out of their homes and cities—and carried captives to Assyria, on the southern shores of the Caspian Sea! And then ... LOST FROM VIEW!

"Therefore the Eternal was very angry with Israel, and removed them out of his sight: *there was none left but the tribe of Judah only*" (II Kings 17:18).

The Eternal removed who? Israel! It is *Israel* which was removed and driven from the Eternal's sight until they became lost from view.

Who was left? Judah ONLY—*only* the Jews! Israel was now gone! They became known as the LOST Ten Tribes and are so designated today.

Gentiles Replace the House of Israel

Now notice II Kings 17:22-23: "For the children of Israel walked in all the sins of Jeroboam which he did; they departed not from them; until the Lord *removed Israel out of his sight*, as he had said by all his servants the prophets. So was Israel [not Judah—not the Jews] carried away out of their own land to ASSYRIA unto this day

84

[written about 620 B.C.]." Observe that the people who had the national title "Israel" and the birthright promises, who were not the Jews, were *carried away out of their own land*—Samaria. They left that land—never yet to return!

Now note the following verse of this same passage: "And the king of Assyria brought men from Babylon, and from Cuthah, and from Ava, and from Hamath, and from Sepharvaim, *and placed* THEM *in the cities of Samaria instead of the children of Israel:* and they possessed Samaria, and dwelt in the cities thereof" (II Kings 17:24).

It is these foreigners who were living in the land of Samaria in the time of Christ and who were called Samaritans in the Gospel records. It is well to keep that in mind. For the Samaritans of the New Testament were not in any sense a racial mixture with the Israelites. Only *one* individual—a priest—returned from among the captive Israelites to teach the newly planted Gentiles the corrupted religion of Israel (II Kings 17:27-28).

These people from the land of Babylon, however, did not follow God, nor God's ways, nor His religion. The very next verse shows this: But "every nation [still] made gods of their own . . ." (II Kings 17:29).

The general state religion of the Assyrians and Babylonians was the Chaldean mystery religion. This was the religion of Simon the sorcerer (Acts 8) who believed Philip's miracles, appropriated the name "Christian," and started a *new* counterfeit "Christianity" after the apostle Peter rejected him as being bound in "iniquity"—i.e., "lawlessness." He took the *name* of Christ, rejected God's law, and added licentious false "grace" to the Babylonian mystery religion, calling it "Christianity." This false "Christianity" has deceived millions, down to this present evil generation!

A more detailed account of the captivity of Israel is found in II Kings 18:9-12 and 17:5-18. The house of Israel began to "abide many days without a king" (Hosea 3:4). Since they were the people who carried the title "Israel," it is they, not Judah, who must become *lost* in identity!

Israel, Not Judah, Lost

The Scriptures plainly tell us that *Israel* was to lose its *identity*, its *language*, its *religion*, its *land*, and its *name*.

In Deuteronomy 32:26, God had warned them through Moses: "I said, I would scatter them into corners, I would MAKE THE REMEMBRANCE OF THEM TO CEASE FROM AMONG MEN." That warning *cannot* be applied to the *Jew*! The remembrance of the Jews has not ceased. The remembrance of them could not cease unless their identity and name were lost. This applies to the LOST tribes, not to the Jews.

Now notice Isaiah 8:17: "And I will wait upon the Lord, THAT HIDETH HIS FACE FROM THE HOUSE OF JACOB." Jacob's name was changed to Israel. In other words, this applies to the house of Israel—the ten-tribed kingdom—who were cut off from the presence of God. They consequently lost the knowledge of the true God, and the true religion.

The Eternal would cease speaking to them in their own Hebrew tongue, but with "another tongue will he speak to *this people*" (Isa. 28:11). This cannot apply to the Jews, who still read their Bibles in the Hebrew tongue.

Isaiah 62:2: "And the Gentiles shall see thy righteousness, and all kings thy glory [after Christ returns]: and thou shalt be called by a NEW NAME, which the mouth of the Lord shall name." While this prophecy

86

refers directly to the future, after Christ's return, it has also been fulfilled, *typically*, foreshadowing that time, by the fact that Israel is known by a different name today. That cannot apply to the Jews. They were known then, and today, as Jews.

Israel Never Returned

The house of Israel did *not* return to Palestine with the Jews in the days of Ezra and Nehemiah, as some erroneously believe. Those who returned to rebuild the Temple and restore worship in Jerusalem at that time, 70 years after *Judah's* captivity, were only those of the house of Judah whom Nebuchadnezzar had carried to Babylon.

Note well these facts.

1) In 721-718 B.C. ISRAEL began to be "carried away out of their own land to Assyria" (II Kings 17:23). They were soon all removed—completely. "There was none left but the tribe of Judah only" (II Kings 17:18). JUDAH, *only, remained.*

2) More than 130 years later, Nebuchadnezzar of Babylon carried the Jews—Judah—who only remained in Palestine away to Babylon. So *none* of the house of Israel dwelt in Palestine at the time of this captivity of Judah.

3) Those who *returned* to Palestine to rebuild the Temple and restore worship 70 years after Judah's captivity were ALL of the house of Judah—*all* JEWS—all of those whom Nebuchadnezzar had carried away. They returned again "unto Jerusalem and Judah, *every one unto his city*" (Ezra 2:1).

Only those of the tribe of Judah, together with remnants of Benjamin and Levi, who constituted the house of Judah, returned at that time. "Then rose up the chief of the fathers of *Judah* and *Benjamin*, and the priests, and the *Levites*" (Ezra 1:5).

THE UNITED STATES AND BRITAIN IN PROPHECY

There are, of course, those who *reject* this truth God has seen fit now, in our time, to reveal—and who falsely represent that ALL Israelites, including the ten-tribed house of Israel, returned to Jerusalem at the time of Ezra and Nehemiah.

They will sift out instances where the word "Israel" is used in connection with individuals or people of the HOUSE OF JUDAH and misrepresent that they are the HOUSE OF ISRAEL. Let it be repeated for emphasis: Jews *are* Israelites—but only *part* of the Israelites are Jews. The term "Jew" is a nickname for the *national* name JUDAH. Jews are, truly, *men of Israel—or people of Israel*—but they are not of the NATION called the HOUSE OF ISRAEL, or KINGDOM OF ISRAEL.

Those who refuse this truth turn to such a passage as this: "And the residue of Israel, of the priests, and the Levites, were in all the cities of Judah, every one in his inheritance" (Neh. 11:20). Because the word "Israel" is used, they will claim these are all twelve tribes. But it is specifically speaking of priests and Levites—and they are of the *house of Judah*, but not of the ten-tribed house of Israel. They were truly the "residue of Israel"— the "residue" of the twelve tribes; they were Israelites, but they were not of the nation called the house of Israel. They returned to their inheritance in the land of *Judah*.

Nehemiah says plainly: "These are the children of the province, that went up out of the captivity [the captivity to Babylon—captivity of JUDAH, *not* the house of *Israel*], of those that had been carried away, whom Nebuchadnezzar the king of Babylon had carried away . . ." (Neh. 7:6). And *none* of the Ten Tribes had been left in Palestine after the Assyrian captivity more than 100 years before (II Kings 17:18).

Ezra says: "And the children of Israel, the priests,

88

and the Levites, and the rest of the children of the captivity, kept the dedication . . ." (Ezra 6:16). These were people of the kingdom of Judah—*not* the kingdom of Israel—but they were "children of Israel."

Names and genealogies are given in Ezra and Nehemiah of those who went back to Palestine from Babylon—and there was *none* from any of the Ten Tribes! Consequently those in Jerusalem at the time of Christ were of these three tribes, *not* of the house of Israel. And most, if not all, of those converted were of the tribe of Benjamin, as Paul said he was.

The house of Israel became known as the LOST Ten Tribes! Now known by *another* name, speaking a different language!

By what name are they known today? Whoever they are, wherever they are, it is *they*, and not the Jews, who are the birthright possessors. It is *they*, not the Jews, who, after the ending of their punishment in A.D. 1800-1803, must inherit the UNbreakable promises to Abraham of national greatness, resources, wealth and power. It is Manasseh who was to become the world's greatest single nation; Ephraim a great *commonwealth* of nations! Who can they be today?

7

Jeremiah's Mysterious Commission

WE COME NOW TO ONE OF THE most fascinating and gripping phases of this strange story of Israel—indeed, the very connecting link between prophecy and present-day fulfillment—yet totally unrecognized by theologians.

After the house of Israel, the northern kingdom whose capital was Samaria, was driven into Assyrian captivity, 721-718 B.C., the Kingdom of JUDAH continued on in the southern part of Palestine known as Judea. At that time Judah, as a nation, had not yet rejected the government and religion of God. God had continued to keep His covenant with David. David's dynasty had continued on the throne over *part* of the Israelites—the house of JUDAH—the Jews.

But after Israel had become lost from view, Judah turned from the ways and government of God, going after the ways of the Gentile nations, sinning even worse than Israel, until finally the Eternal drove Judah, too, into national captivity and slavery.

Before Judah's apostasy, God had said, through the prophet Hosea: "Though thou, ISRAEL, play the harlot, yet let not JUDAH offend . . ." (Hosea 4:15). But later, the Eternal said to Jeremiah: "Have you seen what she did, that faithless one, ISRAEL, how she . . . played the harlot? . . . and her false sister JUDAH saw it. She saw that for all the adulteries of that faithless one, ISRAEL, I had sent her away with a decree of divorce; yet her false sister JUDAH did not fear, but *she too* went and played the harlot . . . . Faithless ISRAEL has shown herself less guilty than false JUDAH" (Jer. 3:6-11, RSV).

Here, again, it is made distinctly plain that the 12 tribes of Israel were divided into two totally separate nations. And yet opponents of the truth revealed in this book deny these plain scriptures—and attempt to discredit those who reveal it.

Now see how Judah (the Jews)—more than 130 years after ISRAEL's captivity—also was removed from their land. They were taken as slaves to Babylon—*not* to Assyria, where ISRAEL had been taken.

"And the Eternal said, I will remove JUDAH *also* out of my sight, as I have removed ISRAEL, and will cast off this city Jerusalem which I have chosen, and the house of which I said, My name shall be there" (II Kings 23:27).

And so, more than 130 years after Israel's captivity, the time came when God caused the Jews also to be driven out of their land in national captivity and slavery.

Jeremiah's Strange Commission

For this purpose God raised up a very special prophet whose real call and commission few indeed understand. This prophet was Jeremiah. Jeremiah played a strange and little realized role in this captivity.

Something of the importance of this mission may be gleaned from this significant fact: The Bible mentions three men only who were sanctified for their respective offices before they were born—and of these three Jeremiah was the first. The other two were John the Baptist and Jesus Christ!

The Eternal first spoke to Jeremiah when he was but a young lad about, some evidence indicates, seventeen years of age. By the time his mission was completed he was an aged, white-haired patriarch.

This vital yet little-known call and commission is described in the opening verses of the first chapter of the book of Jeremiah. "Before I formed you in the womb I knew you," the Eternal said to him, "and before you were born I consecrated you; I appointed you a prophet to the nations" (Jer. 1:5, RSV).

But Jeremiah was frightened—afraid! "Ah, Eternal God!" he replied. "Behold, I do not know how to speak, for I am only a youth."

But the Eternal answered, "Do not say, 'I am only a youth'; for to all to whom I send you you shall go, and whatever I command you you shall speak. Be not afraid of them, for I am with you to deliver you" (verses 6-8).

Then the Eternal put forth His hand and touched Jeremiah's mouth. "See," said God, "I have set you this day *over nations* and over kingdoms, *to pluck up and to break down, to destroy and to overthrow,* TO BUILD AND TO PLANT" (verses 9-10). Or, as this tremendous commission is worded in the Authorized Version: "to root out, and to pull down, and to destroy, and to throw down, to BUILD, AND TO PLANT."

Notice, Jeremiah was set over NATIONS—more than one kingdom. He was a Jewish lad, living in Judah. He was set a prophet over Judah—but not Judah *alone*. Over NATIONS—over KINGDOMS! He was set over these kingdoms to do *two* things: first, to "pluck up," or "root out," to "pull down," or to "overthrow," and second, TO BUILD, AND TO PLANT.

Not Realized Today

Look at it in your own Bible! Jeremiah was used of God as a prophet to warn the nation Judah of their transgressions against God's government and ways. He was sent to warn this rebellious nation of impending punishment—their invasion and captivity at the hands of the Chaldean armed forces—unless they acknowledged their guilt and changed their ways. He was used as a go-between—an intermediary—between the kings of Judah and Babylon.

It is well known that Jeremiah was used in warning Judah of the impending captivity, and the "pulling down" or "overthrowing" of *the throne of David* in the Kingdom of Judah.

It is generally understood that the house of Judah was invaded by the armies of King Nebuchadnezzar; that the Jews were taken captive to Babylon; that they ceased from being a kingdom; that there no longer existed a ruler of David's dynasty on the throne over the Kingdom of Judah.

What, then, does this mean? Did God, at last, forget His covenant promise to David that David's dynasty should *never cease*—that David's throne was established in Solomon to continue through ALL GENERATIONS FOREVER? Had God Almighty now forgotten that He had sworn that He would not alter this promise—even though the kings and the people rebelled and sinned? The faithfulness of GOD is at stake. The inspiration of the Holy Bible as His revealed WORD is at stake!

But note it! See it in your own Bible! Jeremiah was divinely commissioned to *pull down* and to *overthrow* that very throne of David in Judah—but notice the second half of the commission. To BUILD AND TO PLANT! To build and to plant WHAT?

Why, naturally, that which he was used in "rooting out" of Judah—the THRONE OF DAVID which God swore He would preserve forever! Jeremiah was set over not just the *one* nation, Judah—but over NATIONS. Over THE KINGDOMS—the Kingdom of Israel as well as Judah!

"See, I have this day set thee over the nations and over the kingdoms, to root out, and to pull down, and to destroy, and to throw down, to build, and to plant."

(Jeremiah 1:10)

He was used in "rooting out" that throne from Judah. Then what was Jeremiah commissioned to do in *Israel?* Notice the *second* half of his strange and little-understood commission—to BUILD and to PLANT!

So far as the world knows, the last king to sit on that throne of David was Zedekiah of Judah. He was thrown down off the throne and the throne rooted out of Judah in the year 585 B.C.—nearly 600 years before Christ!

What happened to that throne? Where was that throne between 585 B.C. and the time of Christ, 600 years

94

later? We know Jeremiah did not plant and REBUILD it in Babylon. God had promised that David's throne should rule over ISRAELITES through *all* generations—not over Gentiles. We have the history of the continuance of the Gentile throne in Babylon.

David's throne was never again planted or built among the Jews! It was not reigning over the Jews in the time of Christ. The Jews were then under the Roman rule. Jesus did not ascend any such throne. The throne was not functioning in Judah—it was not existing at that place or over that people—it was not there for Jesus to take over. And Jesus said plainly that HIS Kingdom *was not of this present age!* Yet He was born to sit upon this very THRONE OF HIS FATHER DAVID (Luke 1:32)!

But that throne was divinely commissioned to be planted and REBUILT by the prophet Jeremiah—*during his lifetime!* Jeremiah was set over *both* Judah and Israel. To be used in *rooting out* David's throne in Judah. But more! To plant and to build, then, of necessity, among the house of ISRAEL, lo, these many days without a king—among LOST Israel, now supposing herself to be GENTILE! Therefore the identity and location of the replanting *must remain hidden to the world until this time of the* END in which we live.

Tearing Down the Throne

The life and work of Jeremiah is a most fascinating story. The first chapters of the book of Jeremiah are devoted to his ministry, warning of the impending captivity of the Jews. He warned the kings, the priests, prophets and people of Judah, delivering God's message. They threw him in prison—and they refused to heed or obey God. Then God caused their captivity.

It is generally known that Babylon took Judah in three different stages. The first siege was in 604 B.C., a

95

date about two years later than has been commonly reckoned, but a date now firmly established. The land did not *completely* pass into the hands of these Gentile Babylonians, however, until a full time-cycle of 19 years later, or 585 B.C. You can read the part played by Jeremiah in this captivity in the book of Jeremiah.

But now notice an interesting fact. The last and final king recorded either in Bible or secular history as having sat on the throne of David was King Zedekiah of Judah. Remember his name. Now notice II Kings 24:18: "Zedekiah was twenty and one years old when he began to reign, and he reigned eleven years in Jerusalem. And his mother's name was Hamutal, the daughter of Jeremiah of Libnah."

Now notice briefly a description of the final tearing down and rooting out of this throne of David: "In the ninth year of Zedekiah king of Judah, in the tenth month, came Nebuchadrezzar king of Babylon and all his army against Jerusalem, and they besieged it. And in the eleventh year of Zedekiah, in the fourth month, the ninth day of the month, the city was broken up. . . . And it came to pass, that when Zedekiah the king of Judah saw them, and all the men of war, then they fled. . . . But the Chaldeans' army pursued after them, and overtook Zedekiah in the plains of Jericho: and when they had taken him, they brought him up to Nebuchadnezzar king of Babylon to Riblah in the land of Hamath, where he gave judgment upon him. Then the king of Babylon slew the sons of Zedekiah in Riblah before his eyes: also the king of Babylon slew all the nobles of Judah. Moreover he put out Zedekiah's eyes, and bound him with chains, to carry him to Babylon" (Jer. 39:1-7).

In the 52nd chapter, first 11 verses, we find almost a word-for-word description of the same events with the added phrase: " . . . and put him [Zedekiah] in prison TILL THE DAY OF HIS DEATH."

These passages bring out these points:

1) The king of Babylon slew *all the sons* of Zedekiah who were heirs to the throne of David.

2) He also slew all the nobles of Judah so as to leave no possible heirs for that throne.

3) Finally, after putting out Zedekiah's eyes, the king who sat on David's throne was himself taken to Babylon where he died in prison.

4) Thus, as it *appears,* and as the whole world has believed, the throne of David ceased, with no possible heirs, or sons, to keep the dynasty alive. Certain it is that from that day on, the throne never again has existed in Judah, in Jerusalem, or among the Jews!

What About Jeconiah?

It is true that a former king of Judah was at that time in the dungeons of Babylon—and he had sons to continue David's line. Former King Jeconiah (Jehoiachin), taken to Babylon in chains, was restored to honor 37 years after the captivity (see II Kings 25:27-30). He was even given the title "king" along with numerous other captive, vassal "kings."

One of Jeconiah's sons was Salathiel, who was the father of Zorobabel, the son of royal seed through whom Jesus Christ Himself traced His royal ancestry back to David! (Matt. 1:12.) And Zorobabel—or Zerubbabel— was the man God caused Cyrus, king of Persia, to make a decree giving him the *governorship*—not the crown of a king—to return to Jerusalem and rebuild the House of God, the Temple, *seventy* years after the captivity.

Yet neither Jeconiah nor any of his sons or grandsons reigned as king in Judah. Why?

If there was a descendant of the line of David who

lived through the captivity, why wasn't he restored to the throne when he was returned to Jerusalem? *Why?* Simply because God would not permit it!

It is God who makes kings—and *unmakes* them! God was determined to remove the crown of David from the ruling line of Pharez and place it on the head of a son of Zarah. Yet a royal line straight from David had to remain in the area so the Christ could be born of David's seed yet hundreds of years in the future. And God also had to keep His promise to David that he, David, would never lack a descendant to sit on the throne! Many intricate and fascinating prophecies had to be carried out—some seemingly contradictory—a difficult job to perform, an awesome commission from God to Jeremiah!

"As I live, saith the Lord, though Coniah [Jeconiah] the son of Jehoiakim king of Judah were the signet upon my right hand, yet would I pluck thee thence"! (Jer. 22:24.) God had determined an end for this line of kings. He was removing the *crown*—not permitting Jeconiah's sons to reign on Judah's throne! God was turning over (*overturning*) the throne to another branch of Judah's family.

God told Jeremiah forcefully, "Thus saith the Lord, Write ye this man childless, a man that shall not prosper in his days: for no man of his seed shall prosper, SITTING UPON THE THRONE OF DAVID, AND RULING ANY MORE IN JUDAH"! (Jer. 22:30.)

God spoke! Jeremiah wrote! History was designed and done as God said! Jeconiah had children—God Himself caused this fact to be recorded (see I Chron. 3:17; Matt. 1:12), but as far as the THRONE OF DAVID was concerned HE WAS CHILDLESS—none of his children ever occupied that throne!

The crown had now been removed from the *Pharez line,* uprooted from Judah, any immediate candidates to the throne killed, and Jeconiah incarcerated in a Baby-

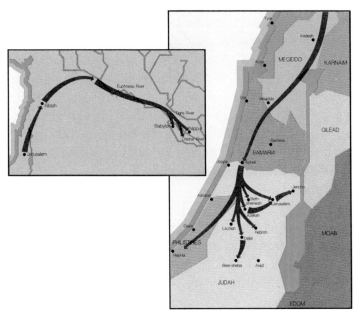

KING NEBUCHADNEZZAR and his army conquered the southern kingdom of Judah and carried its people captive to Babylonia—far to the
south of those areas to which the northern tribes had earlier been
taken by the Assyrians.

lonian prison, written childless as far as the throne was
concerned by the command of God Almighty!

Jeremiah had now accomplished the *first* part of
his great commission. The throne had been rooted out,
the kingdom torn completely down. Judah was now
beginning HER national punishment.

Where Did Jeremiah Go?

But what about the *second* part of Jeremiah's important
commission?

Jeremiah was among these captive Jews. He must
be free to carry out the second part of his commission.

So, "Nebuchadrezzar king of Babylon gave charge
concerning Jeremiah to Nebuzaradan the captain of the

99

guard, saying, Take him, and look well to him, and do him no harm; but do unto him even as he shall say unto thee" (Jer. 39:11-12). "And the captain of the guard took Jeremiah, and said unto him. . . . behold, I loose thee this day from the chains which were upon thine hand. If it seem good unto thee to come with me into Babylon, come; and I will look well unto thee: but if it seem ill unto thee to come with me into Babylon, forbear: behold, all the land is before thee: whither it seemeth good and convenient for thee to go, thither go. . . . So the captain of the guard gave him victuals and a reward [money], and let him go" (Jer. 40:2-5).

So Jeremiah was left absolutely free to do as he pleased, supplied even with expense money, and given complete freedom, so that he might perform the second half of his mission. Where did he go?

We come now to an amazing, fascinating, thrilling part of the book of Jeremiah which has been almost entirely overlooked. "Then went Jeremiah unto Gedaliah the son of Ahikam to *Mizpah*; and dwelt with him among the people that were left in the land" (verse 6).

Now this Gedaliah had been made governor over a remnant of Jews in the land by the king of Babylon, and since Jerusalem was destroyed, he had made Mizpah his headquarters. But the king of Ammon plotted with a Jew named Ishmael to assassinate Gedaliah. The plot was executed; the governor and part of the Jews were slain. Jeremiah was among the survivors.

"Then Ishmael carried away captive all the residue of the people that were in Mizpah, *even the king's daughters*, and all the people that remained in Mizpah, whom Nebuzaradan the captain of the guard [from Babylon] had committed to Gedaliah . . . and carried them away captive, and departed to go over to the Ammonites" (Jer. 41:10).

100

Ah! Did you catch it? Read that passage again. Among these Jews were *the king's daughters!* Daughters of Zedekiah, king of Judah, and of David's dynasty!

King Zedekiah had died in prison in Babylon (Jer. 52:11). All his sons had been killed. All the nobles of Judah had been killed. All possible heirs of Zedekiah to David's throne had been killed—*except the king's daughters!* Now we see why Jeremiah went to Mizpah!

Jeremiah Escapes

Soon a man named Johanan replaced Ishmael as leader. And in fear of reprisals from Nebuchadnezzar and the Chaldean army, Johanan and the captains appealed to the prophet "and said unto Jeremiah the prophet, Let, we beseech thee, our supplication be accepted before thee, and pray for us unto the Lord thy God . . . that the Lord thy God may shew us the way wherein we may walk" (Jer. 42:2-3). They were like so many professing Christians today. They come to God's minister with solemn assurances that they surely do want to know God's will; they promise, as did these, "we will obey the voice of the ETERNAL our God" (verse 6).

But did they mean it? Such people seldom do. Human nature wants to *be* good—or *think* it is good—but it does not want to *do* good.

The word of the Lord came to Jeremiah, and He told them not to fear, that He would protect and deliver them. But the people wanted to flee to Egypt. This the Lord warned them not to do. If they did, the sword of Nebuchadnezzar which they feared would overtake them there, and they would die. "If ye wholly set your faces to enter into Egypt," God said, "and go to sojourn there; then it shall come to pass, that the sword, which ye feared, shall overtake you there . . . and there ye shall die" (Jer. 42:15-16).

But, as people usually do, they rejected God's warning. "Thou speakest falsely," Johanan answered, "the ETERNAL our God hath not sent thee to say, Go not into Egypt" (Jer. 43:2-3). "So Johanan . . . and all the people, obeyed not the voice of the ETERNAL" (verse 4). People who loudly *profess* to want to do God's will usually will not accept God's Word as being His will, unless it is *their* will!

And so Johanan "took all the remnant of Judah . . . even men, and women, and children, *and the king's daughters . . . and Jeremiah the prophet, and Baruch the son of Neriah* [Jeremiah's scribe, or secretary]. So they came into the land of Egypt" (Jer. 43:5-7).

On reaching Egypt, God warned these Jews again through Jeremiah that they should die there by the sword and famine, and "none shall return *but such as shall escape*"! (Jer. 44:12-14.) Yes, a *few* in this company are under divine protection. A divine mission is to be performed. They shall ESCAPE! The Eternal continues: "Yet a small number that escape the sword shall return out of the land of Egypt into the land of Judah" (Jer. 44:28).

Under Divine Protection

Baruch was Jeremiah's constant companion and secretary. It is important to note here God's promise of protection to him: "Thus saith the Lord, the God of Israel, unto thee, O Baruch. . . . Behold, that which I have built will I break down, and that which I have planted I will pluck up, even this whole land. . . . but thy life will I give unto thee for a prey in all places whither thou goest" (Jer. 45:2-5). Baruch's life, like Jeremiah's, was under divine protection!

Now previously the Eternal had said to Jeremiah, "Verily it shall be well with thy REMNANT." The only "remnant" left for Jeremiah's mission of transplanting the throne was the king's daughters. "Verily," continued the Eternal, same verse, "I will cause the enemy to entreat thee well in the time of evil and in the time of affliction" (Jer. 15:11). This God literally did, as described in chapter 39:11-12 and chapter 40:2-6, which I have covered previously.

Notice, it is to be well with the royal material given to Jeremiah with which to build and to plant—and Jeremiah is to be protected and to go to a land that he knows not! Who else was to go to a land they knew not? The ten-tribed birthright kingdom, Israel!

So Jeremiah and his little royal remnant are to escape out of Egypt, return to Judah, and then—where? To the place where the "lost ten tribes" had gone, as we shall see!

Now let Isaiah complete this prophecy: "For out of Jerusalem shall go forth a remnant, and they that escape out of mount Zion: the zeal of the Lord of hosts shall do this. And the remnant that is escaped of the house of Judah shall AGAIN TAKE ROOT DOWNWARD, AND BEAR FRUIT UPWARD" (Isa. 37:32, 31).

This same prophecy is found also in II Kings 19:30-31. It is a prophecy given through Isaiah in the 14th year of the reign of King Hezekiah of Judah, when King Sennacherib of Assyria threatened invasion of Judah. It was a prophecy to happen later—not during Hezekiah's reign. Some critics, seeking to overthrow this basic and important truth, argue that this same remnant is mentioned also in II Chronicles 30:6. But that event is *not* a prophecy, but a historic account of an event in the *first* year of Hezekiah—and *that* remnant did not escape from Jerusalem, but they were Jews who escaped from Sennacherib's forces threatening invasion of Judah— they escaped *into*, not *out of* Judah. And nothing is said here about "taking root downward, and bearing fruit upward," as in both Isaiah 37 and II Kings 19.

This prophecy is so important it is recorded twice! It does refer to the remnant to escape later—to Jeremiah's escape. This remnant with Jeremiah—at least one of the king's daughters—shall *take root downward!* That is, BE REPLANTED!

And then *bear fruit upward!* Be BUILT! Has God failed in His solemn covenant to keep alive David's throne? Where was this planting and building? Can we find it in God's Word? We can! The place and the people among whom the throne was reestablished are clearly identified!

8

The Mysterious Breach

WHERE DID JEREMIAH GO WITH
Baruch his secretary and one or
more of the royal daughters of
the king? History stops short at this point. Enlightened
students of Bible history have long known that the Ten
Tribes—called by the name "house of Israel"—have
been lost in identity and historic knowledge, and exist
today among the Gentile nations, unrecognized. Their
identity and location God has hidden from the world.

Yet, in this end time, when knowledge is to increase, when the "wise" are to *understand* (Dan.
12:4,10), we shall find the secret revealed through
PROPHECY which could not be understood until now. But
first, we must consider a mysterious "breach" that
occurred in the days of Judah, son of Jacob.

Judah was the father of twin sons. The firstborn
was royal seed, for through him the sceptre promise was

105

to be carried down. It seems the midwife knew twins were about to be born. It is recorded that just before birth one of the twins "put out his hand: and the midwife took and bound upon his hand a scarlet thread, saying, This came out first." But the child drew back his hand and the other was actually born first.

The midwife exclaimed, "How hast thou broken forth? this breach be upon thee [margin, wherefore hast thou made this breach against thee?]: therefore his name was called Pharez," meaning "breach." The other twin was named Zarah (Gen. 38:27-30).

Why should this strange occurrence be recorded in Bible history unless this breach was to be *healed* between the sons or their descendants at some future time? Yet it never occurred in their lifetime.

Zarah, of the scarlet thread, had five sons (I Chron. 2:6). Did a descendant of Zarah finally get the throne, in a manner *healing* the breach? David, Zedekiah, Christ—all were of the PHAREZ branch—*none* of Zarah.

Now consider: 1) the *fact* of the breach means the transfer of the sceptre from the Pharez to the Zarah line. 2) Such transfer never occurred before King Zedekiah of Judah, who was descended from Pharez. 3) Therefore it had to occur *after* Zedekiah was dethroned. 4) Since David's line (Pharez) is to *remain* on the throne through all generations forever, it could only occur at an OVERTURN of the throne by a marriage between a Pharez heir to the throne and one of the Zarah line, thus healing the breach.

The Three Overturns

History shows the descendants of Zarah became wanderers, journeying to the north within the confines of the Scythian nations, their descendants later migrating to Ireland in the days of King David.

But meanwhile, the Pharez-David-Zedekiah line

possessed the sceptre—was HIGH—exalted. The Zarah line, feeling it rightfully should possess the sceptre, and some day would, was low, abased—so far as royal power was concerned.

Now consider a much misunderstood passage of prophecy. If you will begin reading at the 18th verse of the 21st chapter of Ezekiel, you will see plainly that the Eternal is here speaking of the captivity of Judah by the king of Babylon. And, beginning in the 25th verse, He says: "And thou, profane wicked prince of Israel [Zedekiah], whose day is come, when iniquity shall have an

"And they slew the sons of Zedekiah before his eyes, and put out the eyes of Zedekiah, and bound him with fetters of brass, and carried him to Babylon."

(II Kings 25:7)

end, thus saith the Lord God; remove the diadem, and take off the crown [as did happen, through the *first* half of Jeremiah's commission]: this [the crown] shall not be the same: *exalt* him that is *low*, and *abase* him that is *high*. I will overturn, overturn, overturn, it: and it shall be no more, until he come whose right it is; and I will give it him."

Let us understand that clearly. "Remove the diadem, and take off the crown." King Zedekiah, of David's dynasty, had the crown. This says it is to be removed. *It was removed.* He died in Babylon; his sons and all the nobles of Judah were killed.

"This shall not be the same." The diadem is not to cease, but a change is to take place—the throne is to be overturned—another is to wear the crown. God's *promise* to David is not to go by default!

"Exalt him that is low, and abase him that is high." Who is "high"? King Zedekiah of Judah. Now he is to be abased. He is to lose that crown. Judah has been "high," while Israel has been "low"—these many years without a king (Hosea 3:4). The Pharez line has been "high"; the Zarah line "low."

"I will overturn, overturn, overturn, it: and it shall be no more, until he come whose right it is." What was to be overturned? The diadem, and the throne. Not once—it is to be overturned *three times.* Overturned by abasing Zedekiah, the house of Judah, the Pharez line, and exalting, now, the house of Israel, and one of the Zarah line! The first of the three overturns was performed as the first half of Jeremiah's commission.

"And it shall be no more." Does this mean the throne—the crown—is to cease to exist? Not at all! How could it be overturned *two more times*—that is, TRANSFERRED from one to another, if it ceased to exist? How, after these three transfers of the crown, could it be given to Him—Christ—whose right it is, at His second coming, if it ceased altogether to exist? How could he who was "low" now be exalted by the crown, if that crown was to be no more? No, the meaning is: "It shall be no more *overturned* until the second coming of Christ"! And then it shall be given to Him!

God will not break His unalterable promise made to

David! Through every generation David shall have a descendant wearing that crown! The *second* half of Jeremiah's commission must now be performed. That throne must be transPLANTED, and again BUILT. The crown must be overturned—*transferred* to another! But WHERE? To WHOM?

A "Riddle" and a "Parable" Tell!

The strange truth of the PLANTING and the REBUILDING of David's throne is revealed in "a riddle and a parable" couched in symbolic language never understood until this latter day. Yet it stands today so clearly explained a little child could understand!

It fills the 17th chapter of Ezekiel's prophecy. The whole chapter should be carefully read. Notice, first, this prophetic message is addressed, NOT to Judah, the Jews, but to the house of Israel. It is a message to give light to the lost ten-tribed house of ISRAEL in these latter days!

First, Ezekiel is told to speak a riddle, and then a parable. The riddle is found in verses 3 to 10. Then, beginning in verse 11, the Eternal explains its meaning. "Say now to the rebellious house [God says, the "rebellious house," being ten-tribed ISRAEL (Ezek. 12:9), to whom Ezekiel is sent a prophet (Ezek. 2:3; 3:1, etc.)], Know ye not what these things mean? tell them . . . " and then the riddle is clearly explained.

A great eagle came to Lebanon and took the highest branch of the cedar. This is explained to represent King Nebuchadnezzar of Babylon who came to Jerusalem and took captive the king of Judah. The cropping off of the cedar's young twigs and carrying them to a land of traffic is explained to picture the captivity of the king's sons. "He took also of the seed of the land" means Nebuchadnezzar took also of the people, and the mighty of the land of Judah. He "set it as a willow tree. And it grew, and became a spreading vine of low stature" means the Jews were given a covenant whereby, although they were ruled over by the Chaldeans, they might live in peace and grow. The other "great eagle" is explained to represent Pharaoh of Egypt.

Thus the riddle covers the *first* half of Jeremiah's commission. Now notice what is revealed concerning the *second* part—the PLANTING of David's throne! It comes in the parable, verses 22-24: "Thus saith the Lord God; I will also take of the highest branch of the high cedar." From God's own explanation we have learned that the cedar tree represents the nation of Judah; its highest branch is Judah's king. The riddle told us Nebuchadnezzar took the highest branch—the king. The parable now tells us *God*—not Nebuchadnezzar, but *God*—will take *of* the highest branch. Not the branch, but OF the branch—of Zedekiah's children. But Nebuchadnezzar took, and killed, all his SONS.

God, through his prophet Jeremiah, is now going to take OF this highest branch and "SET IT" (verse 22). "I will crop off from the top of his young twigs a *tender one*, and will plant it upon an high mountain and eminent," continues the Almighty! Ah! "A tender young twig"! The twigs of this highest branch represent the children of King Zedekiah! Certainly a tender young twig, then, represents a DAUGHTER! " . . . and will PLANT it." Could symbolic language say plainer this young Jewish princess is to become the royal seed for PLANTING again of David's throne? Where? " . . . upon an high mountain and eminent," says the Eternal! A "mountain" in symbol always represents a NATION.

But Which Nation?

"In the mountain of the height of ISRAEL will I plant it," answers the Eternal! David's throne now is to be planted

110

in ISRAEL, after being thrown down from JUDAH! Could language be plainer? " . . . and it [the tender young twig—the king's daughter] shall bring forth boughs, and bear fruit, and be a goodly cedar."

Did David's throne cease with Zedekiah of Judah? Did God forget His covenant? No! Compare this language with the passage in Isaiah 37:31-32: "The remnant that is escaped of the house of Judah shall again take root downward [be planted], and BEAR FRUIT UPWARD." It was PLANTED in ISRAEL, who removed from Judah! After this Hebrew princess is "planted" on the throne, now in ISRAEL, lost from view—that throne is to BEAR FRUIT. She is to marry, have children, and her sons are to continue David's dynasty!

" . . . and under it shall dwell all fowl of every wing; in the shadow of the branches thereof shall they dwell" (Ezek. 17:23). "Lost" Israel, now having acquired the throne and become again a self-ruling nation, shall, in time, spread around the earth gaining dominance and power. They shall inherit the unconditional promises of the BIRTHRIGHT, according to God's covenant with Abraham!

"And all the trees of the field . . . " (verse 24). A "tree" in this riddle and parable is likened to a nation. In other words, "all the nations of the earth." " . . . shall know that I the Lord have brought down the high tree." Judah, the high tree, having the throne 130 years after Israel had been taken captive, now is brought down to the low stature of slavery. " . . . have exalted the low tree." For 130 years Israel had been a "low tree." Now Israel is exalted, becomes again a thriving nation with a Davidic king. " . . . have dried up the green tree [Judah], and have made the dry tree [Israel] to flourish."

Compare that language with Ezekiel 21:26: "Remove the diadem, and take off the crown . . . exalt him

111

that is low, and abase him that is high. I will over-turn . . . " etc. It is speaking of transferring the throne from Judah to Israel.

Israel had already been independent in Ireland for four centuries. Israel in Ireland already had a kingly line onto which Zedekiah's daughter was grafted. The Irish Israelites were an ancient colony and had not gone into Assyrian captivity.

ISRAEL, headed by the tribes of Ephraim and Ma-nasseh, who possessed the birthright, now would flour-ish, become prosperous in due time. "I the Lord have spoken and have done it" (Ezek. 17:24).

Yes, that BIRTHRIGHT is in ISRAEL. Though *lost,* though supposed to be a Gentile nation, they are the people who were to grow into the promised multitude— the great nation and the company of nations, possessing the gates of their enemy nations, becoming a colonizing people spreading around the world, being blessed with national resources and wealth. And, when they become thus powerful and nationally dominant, remember, Da-vid's throne will be found transplanted among them!

But where did Jeremiah, with his royal seed for the transplanting, go to find the lost house of Israel? Where are they today? How was the "breach" healed, and how did a son of Zarah ascend the throne? Can we tell?

We CAN! The exact, precise location is revealed in Bible prophecy! We can pick up Jeremiah's trail in actual history besides!

9

Israel's New Land

W E ARE READY NOW TO SEARCH out the actual location of the lost tribes of the outcast house of Israel. We know they exist today as a nation, and a company of nations, powerful, looked upon as Gentiles. And when we find them, we shall find the throne of David!

Many passages of prophecy tell of these people in these latter days. Prophecies not to be understood until this "time of the end." Prophecies containing a message to be carried to these people by those to whom God reveals it!

First, fix in mind these facts:

The prophet Amos wrote, in the days of the 13th of the 19 kings of the house of Israel (Amos 1:1): "Behold, the eyes of the Lord God are upon the sinful kingdom [house of Israel—Judah had not yet sinned], and I will destroy it [the kingdom, or government, not the people]

113

from off the face of the earth. . . . For, lo, I will command, and I will sift the house of Israel among all nations, like as corn is sifted in a sieve, yet shall not the least grain fall upon the earth" (Amos 9:8-9).

This prophecy usually is applied to the scattered condition of the Jews. But it has nothing to do with the Jews, or house of Judah, but refers to the ten-tribed house of ISRAEL—driven to Assyrian captivity, then migrating from there and scattering among other nations *before* the Jews were taken to Babylon. This prophecy says that ISRAEL (not Judah) was to be sifted among other nations—these Israelites losing their identity—yet God has protected and kept them: "yet shall not the least grain fall upon the earth."

A New Homeland

It was during this time that the children of the house of Israel were to "abide many days without a king" (Hosea 3:4). That these people did sift through all nations is clear. Many New Testament passages indicate this. Although many of them still were scattered among various nations in the first century A.D., a portion of them had become established in a definite location of their own by Jeremiah's time—140 years after their original captivity.

But these Israelites who possessed the birthright eventually were to come to a new land of their own. The Eternal says, in II Samuel 7:10 and I Chronicles 17:9: "Moreover I will appoint a place for my people Israel, and will PLANT THEM [Jeremiah was commissioned to do the PLANTING of the throne among them], that they may dwell in a place of their own, and *move no more.*" The context of the whole passage shows this refers, not to Palestine, but a different land where these scattered Israelites were to gather after being removed from the

114

promised land of Palestine, while that land was lying idle and in possession of the Gentiles.

Notice carefully! After being removed from Palestine, being sifted among all nations, abiding many days without a king, losing their identity, they are to be "planted" in a faraway strange land now to become their own. And, note it, after reaching this place *they are to move no more!* That is, of course, during this present world.

While other prophecies indicate these birthright holders were to become a colonizing people, spreading around the world, it is plain that the spreading out must be from this appointed place, which must remain the "home" seat of government for David's throne.

Mark this clearly! Once this "place of their own" was reached, and the throne of David planted there, THEY WERE TO MOVE NO MORE. Therefore, the location of this people today is the place where Jeremiah planted David's throne more than 2500 years ago!

Therefore prophecies pertaining to *this* day, or to the location of this people just prior to Christ's return, will tell us the location of Jeremiah's planting. The house of Israel is *yet* to return, at Christ's coming, to Palestine—yet to plant grapes in Samaria, their original country. Prophecies telling where they shall, in that future day, migrate FROM will reveal the location of "lost" ten-tribed ISRAEL! The two succeeding "overturns" of the throne, too, must be located in this same general locale.

Lost Israel Located

Without further suspense, let us see where prophecy locates these birthright holders, now possessing the throne of David and having received earth's richest national blessings. Remember they are distinguished

115

from Judah—the Jews—by various names: "Ephraim," "Joseph," "Jacob," "Rachel" (the mother of Joseph), "Samaria" (their former home), "Israel."

According to Hosea 12:1: "Ephraim . . . followeth after the east wind." An "east wind" travels west. Ephraim must have gone *west* from Assyria. When the Eternal swore to David that He would perpetuate his throne, He said: "I will *set* his hand [sceptre] also *in the sea*" (Ps. 89:25). The throne is to be "set," planted, "in the sea."

Through Jeremiah the Eternal said: "Backsliding Israel hath justified herself more than treacherous Judah. Go and proclaim these words *toward the* NORTH, and say, Return, thou backsliding Israel, saith the Lord" (Jer. 3:11-12). Israel is clearly distinguished from Judah. Of course Israel was north of Judah while still in Palestine—but when these words were written by Jeremiah, Israel had been removed from Palestine more than 130 years and had long since migrated, *with* the Assyrians, north (and west) of Assyria's original location.

And in these last days messengers are to go "toward the NORTH" (of Jerusalem) in order to locate lost Israel and proclaim this warning. So the location, we now find, is toward the north, also west, and in the sea.

The 18th verse, same chapter, says: "In those days the house of Judah shall walk with the house of Israel [margin, *to* the house of Israel], and they shall come together *out of the land of the north* to the land that I have given for an inheritance unto your fathers." At the future exodus, at Christ's coming, they are to return to Palestine out of the land of the NORTH!

After saying, "How shall I give thee up, Ephraim?" the Eternal, speaking through Hosea, says: "Then the children shall tremble from the west" (Hosea 11:8, 10).

116

Again: "Behold, I will bring them from the north country, and gather them from the coasts of the earth" (Jer. 31:8). This prophecy is for consideration in the "latter days" (Jer. 30:24; 31:1), and is addressed to "Israel" (verses 2, 4, 9), to "Ephraim" (verses 6, 9), and "Samaria" (verse 5). Here is added another hint—"the coasts of the earth" (verse 8)—evidencing they are dominant at sea and indicating they have spread abroad widely by colonization.

Referring to the house of ISRAEL, not Judah (Isaiah 49:3,6), God says: "Behold, these shall come from far: and, lo, these *from the* NORTH *and from the* WEST; and these from the land of Sinim" (Isa. 49:12). In the Hebrew, the language in which this was originally inspired, there is no word for "northwest," but this term is designated by the phrase, "the north and the west." It means, literally, the northwest! The Vulgate renders "Sinim" as "Australi," or "Australia." So we now have the location *northwest of Jerusalem* and even spreading around the world.

Hence, Israel of TODAY—Israel of the day of Jeremiah's "planting" of David's throne—is located specifically as northwest of Jerusalem and in the sea! Let us locate this land more specifically!

The same 49th chapter of Isaiah begins with this: "Listen, O isles, unto me." The people addressed, Israel, are called "O isles" in the first verse and "O Israel" in the third verse. This term "isles" or "islands" is sometimes translated "coastlands."

The 31st chapter of Jeremiah, locating Israel in the "north country," says: "I am a father to Israel, and Ephraim is my firstborn. Hear the word of the Lord, O ye nations [Ephraim, Manasseh], and declare it *in the isles* afar off . . . " (Jer. 31:9-10).

Again: "Keep silence before me, O islands. . . . thou,

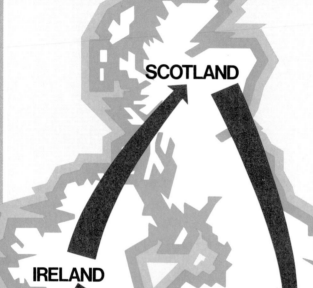

Israel, art my servant, Jacob whom I have chosen"
(Isa. 41:1, 8).

In Jeremiah 31:10, the message is to be declared "in
the isles afar off" and is to be shouted in "the CHIEF OF
THE NATIONS" (verse 7). So, finally, today, as in Jeremiah's day, the house of Israel is in the isles, which are
"in the sea," the chief of the nations, northwest of Jerusalem. A coast-dwelling, and therefore sea-dominant,
people. Certainly there can be no mistaking that identity!

Take a map of Europe. Lay a line due NORTHWEST of
Jerusalem across the continent of Europe, until you
come to the sea, and then to the islands in the sea! This
line takes you directly to the British Isles!

Of proof that our white, English-speaking peoples
today—Britain and America—are actually and truly the
birthright tribes of Ephraim and Manasseh of the "lost"
house of Israel there is so much we shall have space for
but a small portion in this book.

Britain's Hebrew Names

A most interesting fact is the Hebrew meaning of the
names of the British people. The house of Israel is the
covenant people. The Hebrew word for "covenant" is
beriyth, or *berith*. After Gideon's death, Israel followed the false pagan god Baal. In Judges 8:33 and
9:4, the word "covenant" is used as a proper name
coupled with the name "Baal." This is quoted in the
English text, Authorized Version, without being translated, as "Baalberith," meaning (margin) "idol of the
covenant."

The Hebrew for "man" is *iysh*, or *ish*. In English,
the ending "-ish" means "*of* or *belonging to* (a spec-
ified nation or person)." In the original Hebrew language vowels were never given in the spelling. So,

119

omitting the vowel "e" from *berith*, but retaining the "i" in its anglicized form to preserve the "y" sound, we have the anglicized Hebrew word for covenant, *brith*.

The Hebrews, however, never pronounced their "h's." Many a Jew, even today, in pronouncing the name "Shem," will call it "Sem." Incidentally, this ancient Hebrew trait is also a modern British trait. So the Hebrew word for "covenant" would be pronounced, in its anglicized form, as *brit*.

And the word for "covenant man," or "covenant people," would therefore be simply "BRIT-ISH." And so, is it mere coincidence that the true covenant people today are called the "BRITISH"? And they reside in the "BRITISH ISLES"!

The house of Israel not only was to lose its identity, but its name. It was to be called by a new name, since they no longer were to know their identity as Israel, as God said plainly in Isaiah 62:2, referring to these latter days, and to the millennium.

To Abraham God said, "In ISAAC shall thy seed be called," and this name is repeated in Romans 9:7 and Hebrews 11:18. In Amos 7:16 the Israelites are called "the house of ISAAC". They were descended from Isaac, and therefore are Isaac's sons. Drop the "I" from "Isaac" (vowels are not used in Hebrew spelling), and we have the modern name "SAAC'S SONS," or, as we spell it in shorter manner, "SAXONS"!

Dr. W. Holt Yates says, "The word 'Saxons' is derived from the 'sons of Isaac,' by dropping the prefix 'I.' "

Many confuse the Anglo-Saxons with the German or Old Saxons who still live in Germany. The German Saxons derive their name from an Old High German word, *Sahs*, meaning "sword" or "knife." These sword-

120

carrying Germans are an entirely different people from the Anglo-Saxons who migrated to Britain.

Dan a Serpent's Trail

As the Eternal intended that "lost" Israel was to be located and found in these last days, we should expect some kinds of signs or waymarks to have been left along the trail by which ancient Israel journeyed from Assyria, the land of their original captivity.

Speaking to Ephraim (verse 20), the Eternal says in Jeremiah 31:21: "Set thee up waymarks, make thee high heaps: set thine heart toward the highway, even the way which thou wentest." In Scripture we find the "waymarks," or highway signs, which they set up along the road they traveled.

In Genesis 49:17, Jacob, foretelling what should befall each of the tribes, says: "Dan shall be a serpent by the way." Another translation of the original Hebrew is: "Dan shall be a serpent's trail." It is a significant fact that the tribe of Dan, one of the Ten Tribes, named every place they went after their father Dan.

The tribe of Dan originally occupied a strip of coast country on the Mediterranean, west of Jerusalem. "And the coast of the children of Dan," we read in Joshua 19:47, "went out too little for them: therefore the children of Dan went up to fight against Leshem, and took it . . . and called Leshem, DAN, after the name of Dan their father."

In Judges 18:11-12, it is recorded that Danites took Kirjath-jearim, and "called that place Mahaneh-*dan* unto this day." A little later the same company of 600 armed Danites came to Laish, captured it, and "they called the name of the city DAN, after the name of Dan their father" (verse 29). So notice how these

121

Keystone Photos

THE OLD CORONATION CHAIR, at right, in Westminster Abbey, London. Under it lies a stone, said to have been brought to Ireland by Jeremiah the prophet and upon which many kings of Scotland and England have been coronated.

Danites left their "serpent's trail" by the way—set up waymarks by which they may be traced today.

Remember, in the Hebrew, vowels were not written. The sound of the vowels had to be supplied in speaking. Thus, the word "Dan" in its English equivalent could be spelled, simply, "Dn." It might be pronounced as "Dan," or "Den," or "Din," or "Don," or "Dun"—and still could be the same original Hebrew name.

The tribe of Dan occupied two different districts, or provinces, in the Holy Land before the Assyrian captivity. One colony lived on the seacoast of Palestine. They were principally seamen, and it is recorded Dan abode in ships (Judges 5:17).

When Assyria captured Israel, these Danites struck out in their ships and sailed west through the Mediterranean and north to Ireland. Just before his death,

122

Moses prophesied of Dan: "Dan is a lion's whelp: he shall leap from Bashan" (Deut. 33:22). Along the shores of the Mediterranean they left their trail in "Den," "Don," and "Din."

Irish annals and history show that the new settlers of Ireland, at just this time, were the "Tuatha de Danaans," which means, translated, "Tribe of Dan." Sometimes the same appears simply as "Tuathe De," meaning the "people of God." And in Ireland we find they left these "waymarks": *Dan*-Laugh, *Dan*-Sower, *Dun*-dalk, *Dun*-drum, *Don*-egal Bay, *Don*-egal City, *Dun*-gloe, *Din*-gle, *Dun*smor (meaning "more Dans"). Moreover, the name Dunn in the Irish language means the same as Dan in the Hebrew: judge.

But the northern colony of Danites was taken to Assyria in the captivity, and thence with the rest of the Ten Tribes they traveled from Assyria by the overland route.

After leaving Assyrian captivity, they inhabited for some time the land just west of the Black Sea. There we find the rivers *Dnieper*, *Dn*iester, and the *Don*.

Then, in either ancient or later geography, we find these waymarks: *Dan*-au, the *Dan*-inn, the *Dan*-aster, the *Dan*-dari, the *Dan*-ez, the *Don*, the *Dan*, and the U-*don*; the Eri-*don*, down to the *Danes*. *Denmark* means "Dan's mark."

When they came to the British Isles, they set up the "waymark" names of *Dun*-dee, *Dun*-raven; in Scotland the "Dans," "Dons" and "Duns" are as prolific as in Ireland. And so the "serpent's trail" of Dan sets up waymarks that lead directly to the British Isles!

Ancient Annals of Ireland

Now briefly let us consider what is found in the ancient annals, legends, and history of Ireland, and we shall have the scene of Jeremiah's "planting" and the present location of "lost" Israel.

The real ancient history of Ireland is very extensive, though colored with some legend. But with the facts of biblical history and prophecy in mind, one can easily sift out the legend from the true history in studying ancient Irish annals. Throwing out that which is obviously legendary, we glean from various histories of Ireland the following: Long prior to 700 B.C. a strong colony called "Tuatha de Danaan" (tribe of Dan) arrived in ships, drove out other tribes, and settled there. Later, in the days of David, a colony of the line of Zarah arrived in Ireland from the Near East.

Then, in 569 B.C. (date of Jeremiah's transplanting), an elderly, white-haired patriarch, sometimes referred to as a "saint," came to Ireland. With him was the princess daughter of an eastern king and a companion called "Simon Brach," spelled in different histories as Breck, Berech, Brach, or Berach. The princess had a Hebrew name Tephi—a pet name—her full name being Tea-Tephi.

Modern literature of those who recognize our national identity has confused this Tea-Tephi, a daughter of Zedekiah, with an earlier Tea, a daughter of Ith, who lived in the days of David.

This royal party included the son of the king of Ireland who had been in Jerusalem at the time of the siege. There he had become acquainted with Tea-Tephi. He married her shortly after 585—when the city fell. Their young son, now about 12 years of age, accompanied them to Ireland. Besides the royal family, Jeremiah brought with them some remarkable things, including a harp, an ark, and a wonderful stone called "lia-fail," or "stone of destiny." A peculiar coincidence (?) is that Hebrew reads from right to left, while English reads from left to right. Read this name either way—and it still is "lia-fail."

Another strange coincidence—or *is* it just coincidence?—is that many kings in the history of Ireland, Scotland, and England have been coronated sitting over this stone—including the present queen. The stone rests today in Westminster Abbey in London, and the coronation chair is built over and around it. A sign beside it labels it "Jacob's pillar-stone" (Gen. 28:18).

The royal husband of the Hebrew princess Tea was given the title Herremon upon ascending the throne of his father. This Herremon has usually been confused with a much earlier Gede the Herremon in David's day—who married his uncle Ith's daughter Tea. The son of this later king Herremon and Hebrew princess continued on the throne of Ireland and *this same dynasty continued unbroken* through all the kings of Ireland; was *overturned* and transplanted again in Scotland; again *overturned* and moved to London, England, where *this same dynasty continues today* in the reign of Queen Elizabeth II.

Another interesting fact is that the crown worn by the kings of the line of Herremon and the other sovereigns of ancient Ireland had *twelve points!*

Queen Elizabeth on David's Throne

In view of the linking together of biblical history, prophecy, and Irish history, can anyone deny that this Hebrew princess was the daughter of King Zedekiah of Judah and therefore heir to the throne of David? That the aged patriarch was in fact Jeremiah, and his companion was Jeremiah's scribe, or secretary, Baruch? That King Herremon was a descendant of Zarah, here married to the daughter of Pharez, healing the ancient breach? That when the throne of David was first overturned by Jeremiah, it was REPLANTED in Ireland, later overturned a second time and replanted in Scotland, overturned a third time and planted in London? When Christ returns to earth to sit on that throne, He shall take over a LIVE, *existing* throne, not a nonexistent one (Luke 1:32).

And the British Commonwealth of Nations is the *only* COMPANY OF NATIONS in all earth's history. Could we so *exactly* fulfill the specifications of the birthright, and not be the birthright people?

The United States expanded rapidly in national resources and wealth after 1800, but reached world dominance among nations later than the British Commonwealth. It became a giant world power by the end of World War I.

The United States Is Manasseh

From the prophetic blessings passed on by the dying Jacob, it is apparent that Ephraim and Manasseh were in a large measure to inherit the birthright jointly; to remain together for a long time, finally separating.

In Genesis 48 Jacob first passed the birthright on to the two sons of Joseph jointly, speaking of them both together. Then, finally, he spoke of them separately— Manasseh was to become the single GREAT nation; Ephraim, the COMPANY of nations.

And in his prophecy for these latter days Jacob said, "Joseph is a fruitful bough, even a fruitful bough by a well; whose *branches run over the wall*" (Gen. 49:22). In other words, Joseph—Ephraim and Manasseh jointly and together—was to be a *colonizing* people in this latter day, their colonies branching out from the British Isles around the earth.

Together Ephraim and Manasseh grew into a multitude, then separated, according to Jacob's prophetic

127

blessing of Genesis 48. Our people have fulfilled this prophecy.

But how can we be Manasseh when a large part of our people have come from many nations besides England? The answer is this: A large part of Manasseh remained with Ephraim until the separation of NEW England. But our forefathers were to be sifted through many nations, as corn through a sieve, yet not a grain to fall to the earth or be lost (Amos 9:9). Our people did filter through many nations. Ephraim and much of Manasseh finally immigrated to England together, but many others of Manasseh who had filtered into and through other nations did not leave them until they came, as immigrants, to the United States AFTER the New England colony had become the separate nation. This does not mean that *all* foreigners who have immigrated into this country are of the stock of Manasseh, but undoubtedly many are. Israel, however, always did absorb Gentiles, who became Israelites through living in Israel's land and intermarrying.

Thus we have become known as the "melting pot" of the world. Instead of refuting our Manasseh ancestry, this fact actually confirms it. The proof that we are Manasseh is overwhelming. Manasseh was to separate from Ephraim and become the greatest, wealthiest single nation of earth's history. We alone have fulfilled this prophecy. Manasseh was in fact a *thirteenth* tribe. There were twelve original tribes. Joseph was one of these twelve. But when Joseph divided into two tribes and Manasseh separated into an independent nation, it became a *thirteenth* tribe.

Could it be mere coincidence that it *started*, as a nation, with *thirteen* colonies?

But what about the *other* tribes of the so-called "Lost Ten Tribes"? While the *birthright* was *Joseph's*, and its blessings have come to the British Commonwealth of Nations and the United States of America, yet the other eight tribes of Israel were also God's chosen people. They, too, have been blessed with a good measure of material prosperity—but *not* the dominance of the birthright.

We lack space for a detailed explanation of the specific identity of all of these other tribes in the nations of our twentieth century. Suffice it to say here that there is ample evidence that these other eight tribes have descended into such northwestern European nations as Holland, Belgium, Denmark, northern France, Luxembourg, Switzerland, Sweden, Norway. The people of Iceland are also of Viking stock. The political boundaries of Europe, as they exist today, do not necessarily show lines of division between descendants of these original tribes of Israel.

10

Birthright Withheld 2520 Years!

T
HE MOST REMARKABLE FULFILL-
ment of biblical prophecy in modern
times was the sudden sprouting
forth of the two mightiest world powers—one, a commonwealth of nations forming the greatest world empire
of all time; the other, the wealthiest, most powerful
nation on earth today. These birthright peoples came,
with incredible suddenness, into possession of more
than two-thirds—nearly three-fourths—of the cultivated wealth and resources of the whole world! This
sensational spurt from virtual obscurity in so short a
time gives incontrovertible PROOF of divine inspiration.
Never, in all history, did anything like it occur.

But why did this unprecedented national wealth
and power come to our birthright inheritors only after
the year A.D. 1800? Why did not this national dominance
come to the tribes of Ephraim and Manasseh millennia

ago—in the days of Moses, or Joshua, or David, or Elijah?

A "Nation" and a "Commonwealth of Nations"

Remember now the birthright promise was given to the two tribes of Ephraim and Manasseh—not to the other tribes or their descendants. These two birthright tribes were part of the northern kingdom of Israel.

Notice again the original promise: "A *nation* and a *company of nations* shall be of thee" (Gen. 35:11).

In passing on the birthright promise the dying Jacob (Israel) said of Ephraim and Manasseh, sons of Joseph, ". . . let *my name* be named on *them*" (Gen. 48:16). Hence it is THEY—the descendants of Ephraim (the British) and Manasseh (Americans)—not the Jews, who are referred to in *prophecy* under the names of *Jacob* or Israel. Continuing, Jacob added, ". . . and let *them* grow into a multitude."

Then, speaking of Manasseh and his descendants *alone*, Jacob said prophetically: ". . . he also shall become a people [nation], and he also shall be GREAT: but truly his younger brother [Ephraim] shall be greater than he, and *his* seed shall become a MULTITUDE [a company, or COMMONWEALTH] of NATIONS" (Gen. 48:19).

In A.D. 1800 the United Kingdom and the United States were small and insignificant among the earth's nations. The United Kingdom consisted only of the British Isles, a very small part of India and of Canada and a few little islands. The United States consisted only of the original 13 colonies and three added states. Neither possessed any great wealth or power.

But beginning in 1800 these two little nations began to sprout and to grow into vast national riches and power such as no people ever possessed. Soon Britain's empire spread around the world, until the sun never set upon her possessions. Canada, Australia, South Africa were given dominion status—made free and independent nations, ruling themselves independent of England—a *company*, or commonwealth, of nations joined together, not by legal government, *but solely by the throne of David!*

But why was that tremendous birthright, which was promised *unconditionally* to Abraham, repromised to Isaac and Jacob, never bestowed for millennia of time— until after A.D. 1800? The answer is amazing—exciting!

To understand this miraculous burst into world dominance, it is necessary to examine the very pivot of Old Testament prophecies—the 26th chapter of Leviticus.

Prophecy for Now

This remarkable prophecy pertains to *our time*, as well as giving warning to the people of Israel in Moses' day. Few realize that the prophecies of the Old Testament pertain, primarily, to this 20th century—not, in many cases, to Old Testament times at all.

Most ministers and church leaders today were schooled in the theological seminaries of their particular denominations. They were taught, nearly altogether, from sectarian books, *not* from the Bible. Many of these will say: "We are a NEW Testament church," supposing Old Testament prophecies pertained only to Old Testament times, having no meaning for us today. *That is an error and a delusion!* Many Old Testament prophecies were never written for, nor read by or to, the Israelites of those times. The New Testament Church of God is actually built on the FOUNDATION of the Old Testament prophets, as well as the apostles (Eph. 2:20).

Daniel wrote after both Israel and Judah had been removed from Palestine as slaves. He had no way to communicate his prophecies to his enslaved country-men—and besides, the meaning was closed and sealed until our time, now (Dan. 12:8-9).

Ezekiel was a prophet, *not* to the Jews of the house of Judah, though he was among them in their captivity. But his prophecy was to be delivered to the house of Israel—driven out some 130 years before, and by Ezekiel's time lost from view. His prophecy was to be delivered to the house of Israel TODAY, in this 20th century, by God's ministers who now *know* their identity!

And this prophecy of Leviticus 26, though written by Moses before the Israelites had entered the promised land, is one of dual fulfillment. It was a *warning* to those of Moses' day, but its final fulfillment, as we shall see, has taken place and is now taking place—in our time. And, through the dual fulfillment, typical of so many prophecies, it is also a WARNING to the American and British peoples of impending events! Leviticus 26 is the basic prophecy of the Old Testament. It contains a vital, living, tremendous message and warning for our people today!

The Pivotal Prophecy

In this central prophecy, God reaffirmed the birthright promise—but with conditions—for those of Moses' day! The birthright tribes of Ephraim and Manasseh were then *with* the other tribes—as one nation. Obedience to God's laws would bring the vast national wealth and blessings of the birthright not only to Ephraim and Manasseh, but the whole NATION would automatically have shared them at that time.

Notice carefully that two of the Ten Commandments are mentioned for emphasis. These were the main *test commandments*! They were the test of obedience, and of faith in and loyalty to God. God said: "Ye shall make you no idols nor graven image . . . to bow down

133

unto it: for *I* am the Eternal your God. Ye shall keep MY sabbaths . . ." (verses 1-2).

There was a *condition*—a great big "if"—to their receiving actual fulfillment of this stupendous birthright promise *in their time!* God said: "*If* ye walk in my statutes, and keep my commandments, and do them; *then* I will give you rain in due season, and the land shall yield her increase . . . " (verses 3-4). All wealth comes out of the ground. They would enjoy bumper crops the year round, one harvest on the heels of another. Verse 6: "And I will give PEACE in the land . . . and none shall make you afraid . . . neither shall the sword [of war] go through your land." What a blessing! What nation enjoys continuous peace, without fear of invasion?

Of course, in this world, every nation has enemies. What if enemy nations attacked? Verses 7-8: "And ye shall chase your enemies, and they shall fall before you by the sword. And five of you shall chase an hundred, and an hundred of you shall put ten thousand to flight. . . ."

Since many nations in this world always have been aggressors, Israel would have been attacked. A nation with the military superiority to defeat all attackers would soon become the dominant, most powerful nation on earth—especially with resources and great wealth from the ground. Verse 9: "For I will have respect unto you, and make you fruitful, and multiply you, and establish my covenant with you."

The Great Big If

But here comes the alternative—*IF* the conditions are not met: ". . . if ye will *not* hearken unto me, and will not

---

THE INDUSTRIAL REVOLUTION brought the birthright tribes to national prominence. Photos show a gold smelter and a steel mill.

135

do all these commandments ... I also will do this unto you; I will even appoint over you terror, consumption, and the burning ague [fever], that shall consume the eyes, and cause sorrow of the heart [RSV: waste the eyes and cause life to pine away]: and ye shall sow your seed in vain, for your enemies shall eat it. And I will set my face against you, and ye shall be slain before your enemies: they that hate you shall reign over you..." (verses 14-17). They would be invaded, conquered, become once again slaves—as they had been in Egypt before God freed them.

Now What Did Happen?

These Israelites griped, grumbled, complained, doubted God almost from the very night they left Egypt. God miraculously delivered them from the pursuing Egyptian army at the Red Sea. God sent manna and quails from heaven to feed them. God caused drinking water to gush from the great rock. But always they complained, showed a rebellious attitude.

The children of Israel, under Moses, came to the desert at the foot of Mount Sinai. There Moses was called up the mountain where God spoke to him. God here offered Israel the opportunity to become HIS NATION—under His rule, and, upon obedience and loyalty to His government, to receive the fabulous national birthright of world dominance.

The ETERNAL said: "Now therefore, If ye will obey my voice indeed, and keep my COVENANT, then ye shall be a peculiar treasure unto me above all people: for all the earth is mine" (Ex. 19:5). Notice, God did not force them to become His nation—a "peculiar" nation, differ-

AN OVER-ABUNDANCE—Top, wheat being poured into streets. That's how great the surplus was! Bottom, air view of giant grain storage bins in the U.S. wheat belt.
Ambassador College Photos

136

BLESSING: VIRTUALLY ENDLESS SUPPLY OF COAL

**BLESSING: STEEL FOR AN ADVANCED
TECHNOLOGY**

Walter Moog Photo

ent from the apostate Gentile kingdoms. The choice was theirs!

The Beginning of a Nation

Moses returned to camp. He laid God's proposed agreement (covenant) before that vast congregation of perhaps two or three million people.

"And all the people answered together, and said, All that the Eternal hath spoken we will do" (verse 8).

For two days the people were specially prepared for a tremendous event. They were to hear the very voice of God from the mountain. On the third day, amid a fantastically tremendous supernatural display of thunder and lightning and thick clouds swirling over the mountain, God's tremendous voice—exceedingly loud—thundered in their ears the *basic law* of His government—the great SPIRITUAL law defining, in principle, GOD's WAY of life—the way to *avoid* the evils besetting the world—the way that would cause peace, happiness, prosperity.

That vast assemblage actually heard the voice of THE ETERNAL GOD, delivering to them the Ten Commandments! The people were frightened! They trembled! It was an awesome experience which had never happened before—and has never occurred since!

Then, through Moses, God outlined in more detail His proposition for setting them up as God's NATION. Again, the people answered with a unanimous voice, "All the words which the Eternal hath said will we do" (Ex. 24:3). Moses wrote all the terms of this COVENANT—this AGREEMENT making these ex-slaves God's nation—this agreement which also was a marriage covenant, with the Eternal as husband, binding the wife (Israel) to obey her husband.

Moses read the terms and conditions—the "book of the covenant"—before all the people. Again came the

142

unanimous decision on their part: "All that the Eternal hath said will we do, and be obedient" (Ex. 24:7).

Old Covenant a Marriage

The covenant agreement between God and this people—called "the old covenant"—was then ratified and put into effect with BLOOD (Ex. 24:5-8).

This "old covenant" was mediated by Moses. It married a mortal, human people to the Eternal. They became HIS NATION. They had promised loyal obedience as citizens. This "old covenant" was based on the birthright promise God had made to Abraham. But human mortals, filled with the vanity, envy, lust and greed of human nature, seldom remain faithful. So the living Christ is now coming soon to be the Mediator of the new covenant, based on better promises (Heb. 8:6-10 and 9:15). But the NEW covenant will not be made with human mortals who do not keep their promises. God has been preparing—and still now is preparing—a people to be made immortal. These immortals are to be married to Christ. And He died, rose, and sent God's HOLY Spirit "that he might sanctify and cleanse" this NEW Testament "wife" (Eph. 5:26-27).

The new covenant will be made with a people who already have been *proved*, by their Christian life of obedience, faith, growing in spiritual character and knowledge, and overcoming—a people *then* made immortal and holy and perfect.

The NEW covenant is based on the *sceptre* promise made to Abraham—through the coming KING of kings, Jesus Christ, of the very dynasty of David.

They Turn to Idolatry

But notice how these mortal Israelites performed.

After the old covenant between God and Israel had

143

BLESSING: FINE HERDS OF CATTLE

Grant Heilman Photo

been ratified, God called Moses up into the mountain. Moses was kept there forty days, receiving detailed instructions for the congregation (church) and for the nation—for with the Israelites church and state were united.

After Moses had been gone some days, the people said to Aaron, "Up, make us gods, which shall go before us; for as for this Moses, the man that brought us up out of the land of Egypt, we wot not what is become of him." So they took their golden earrings and trinkets, and Aaron had them made into a golden calf for an idol (Ex. 32:1-4).

Moses came down from the mount carrying the two tablets of stone on which the Eternal had engraved the Ten Commandments with His own finger. On seeing this golden idol and the people worshiping it in merriment and dancing, he lost his temper and in a rage threw down the tablets of stone and broke them.

Of course, just as some very large religious bodies who claim to be Christian do today, they merely said this calf *represented* God—it pictured to them what they supposed God looked like.

After making this molten gold calf, Aaron proclaimed a feast "to the Eternal" (Ex. 32:5), during which they worshiped before the IDOL. Go into an Anglican church or a Roman Catholic church today and ask the priest or official whether the images of "Christ" and of "Mary" are idols—whether or not they are worshiping IDOLS. They will indignantly say, "No! We don't worship idols. We don't worship the images. We don't claim the images actually *are* Christ or Mary—only that they *represent*, or picture to us, what Christ or Mary look like!"

Well, that is precisely the way ALL PAGANS ALWAYS WORSHIPED IDOLS! But God's wrath waxed HOT at this

146

(Ex. 32:7-10). God will NOT ACCEPT such worship! See also Deuteronomy 12:30-31.

Withheld 40 Years

In the second year after leaving Egypt, God had moved the Israelites to a new camp in the wilderness of Paran (Num. 10:11-12). God then told Moses to send twelve men—one leader or ruler from each tribe—to spy out the promised land and bring back a report on the land and its inhabitants (Num. 13:1-2).

These men were gone 40 days. On their return, all but two—Joshua and Caleb—misrepresented what they had seen, giving an evil report. When Joshua and Caleb reported the truth, the people tried to stone them. They accepted the evil report, complained against God, doubted, rebelled, disobeyed.

Have you ever wondered why these Israelites were *40 years* in the desolate, barren, desert-and-mountain wilderness getting to the promised land? It was not because it required 40 years of travel. These men sent to report on it journeyed to it, walked all over it from one end to the other and returned—round trip—in 40 *days.* But the people griped, disbelieved God, disobeyed, and refused to go forthwith to POSSESS IT; instead of deciding to march ahead and POSSESS this great prize God wanted to give them, they *despised it,* lacked faith to go in and possess it, refused to march forward.

This promised land is a type of the glorious Kingdom of God, which the living Savior, Jesus Christ, offers us. But today we, the descendants of those Israelites, despise it, prefer the "slavery" of SIN, fail to exercise the FAITH to go on and POSSESS God's Kingdom. We, too, rebel, disbelieve, and disobey. And those who thus despise it shall not enter that glorious Kingdom with eternal life in happiness and accomplishment.

147

To this rebellious population, God said: "Your carcases shall fall in this wilderness ... ye shall not come into the land ... save Caleb ... and Joshua. ... But your little ones, which ye said should be a prey, them will I bring in, and they shall know the land which ye have despised" (Num. 14:29-31).

"And," continued God, "your children shall wander in the wilderness *forty years*, and bear your whoredoms, until *your* carcases be wasted in the wilderness" (verse 33).

And now comes the *"day-for-a-year* principle": "After the number of the *days* in which ye searched the land, even *forty days, each day for a year*, shall ye bear your iniquities, even *forty years* ... " (verse 34). And this punishment was, in fact, a WITHHOLDING of the promised blessing for this duration of forty years.

Idolatry Again

That generation of Israelites was not allowed to enter the promised land. They spent forty years in the wilderness. Their children entered the Holy Land under Joshua's leadership.

Then what?

They became so busy occupying their promised land, driving out the many little kingdoms, that during Joshua's life and a little longer they served God and prospered. They were making a nice start toward inheriting—in *their* day—the tremendous blessings of the birthright.

But after Joshua died "and also all that generation ... there arose another generation after them, which knew not the Eternal, nor yet the works which he had done for Israel. And the children of Israel did evil in the sight of the Eternal, and served Baalim: And they forsook the Eternal God of their fathers. ... And the anger of the Eternal was hot against Israel, and he delivered them into the hands of spoilers that spoiled them, and he sold them into the hands of their enemies round about, so that they could not any longer stand before their enemies. Whithersoever they went out, the hand of the Eternal was against them for evil, as the Eternal had said, and as the Eternal had sworn unto them: and they were greatly distressed" (Judges 2:10-15).

So, precisely as God had warned in verses 14-17 of Leviticus 26, God *did* appoint over them terror; they *did* sow their seed in vain, for their enemies ate it. God did set His face against them!

God's WORD STANDS! What a pity neither individuals nor nations seem able to believe that!

But that was not the end. God is a merciful, forgiving God. He repeatedly gave them another chance. Continue the history in the book of Judges: "Nevertheless the Eternal raised up judges, which delivered them out of the hand of those that spoiled them. And yet they would not hearken unto their judges, but they went a whoring after other gods, and bowed themselves unto them: they turned quickly out of the way . . . " (Judges 2:16-17).

This happened repeatedly. Every time they were put under the yoke of another nation, as vassals, they cried out to God for deliverance. But also every time God sent a judge to free them, they quickly turned from God. As soon as things were going well for them, these people turned again to idolatry.

But were they so different from us, their descendants today? Most of us seek God only when in trouble—only when in our *self*-interest we feel we need Him!

Up until this time, though these people had complained, lacked faith, gone contrary to God repeatedly,

149

nevertheless, they still recognized GOD as their only Ruler. They may not have trusted in, or obeyed Him and His rule, but they acknowledged no other Ruler.

They Reject God as King

But in the days of Samuel they rejected God even as their national King—as their civil Ruler. They demanded a human king, like all the unbelieving Gentiles (I Sam. 8:1-7). This probably took place near the end of 1112 B.C.

To reject God as Ruler was the greatest sin. Up until this time they had recognized Him—had looked to no other as King. This seems to have begun the years of complete sin, for which God punished them.

Nevertheless, under the "old covenant" of Mt. Sinai, they were still God's nation. God still dealt with them. He did not "divorce" them until 721-718 B.C., as we shall see.

They suffered under Saul. They began prospering under King David, and in Solomon's reign they reached a considerable state of prosperity. However, they had not yet flowered into the full predominant-world-power status promised under the birthright. And Solomon's prosperity turned him to idolatry. Again they were violating the *condition* for receiving the birthright.

When Solomon's son Rehoboam became king, he threatened to put still heavier tax burdens on the people. Thereupon the nation rejected Rehoboam and set up Jeroboam, of the tribe of Ephraim, as king.

A Nation Divided

This caused division! In order to retain the Davidic dynasty, Judah thereupon seceded. With Benjamin, and most of Levi, they formed a new nation—the kingdom of Judah! No longer did they have the national name "Israel." The people of this new-formed kingdom of Judah are the ones who became known as the Jews. The people of the kingdom of Israel, occupying the northern part of Palestine north of Jerusalem, never were called Jews.

Now the birthright and sceptre promises *were divided* into two nations. Remember, Ephraim and Manasseh shared the birthright. *If* it were then inherited, the others of the ten-tribed nation of Israel would have automatically shared it with them—since they were part of the same nation!

But under Jeroboam the ten-tribed nation Israel completely violated God's laws, particularly the two test commandments. Almost the first act of Jeroboam was setting up idols. And he *changed* God's autumn festivals from the seventh to the eighth month. There is ample evidence that he also changed God's Sabbath from the seventh to the "eighth" day (first day of the week). This will be shown in a later chapter.

Even after all this, God gave the nation every chance to qualify for the tremendous birthright blessings. During the reigns of nineteen kings in seven different dynasties, God pleaded with them through His prophets. But this rebellious nation showed no disposition to turn to God's ways. They had been punished repeatedly. But they refused to learn the lesson experience should have taught them.

The Seven Prophetic Times

Now continue in Leviticus 26: "And if ye will not yet for all this hearken unto me, then I will punish you *seven times* more for your sins" (verse 18).

It is important to UNDERSTAND this!

This expression "*seven times*" is translated into the English from a Hebrew word which conveys a dual meaning. The original Hebrew word Moses wrote is *shibah*. It is defined as "seven times," and also as "sevenfold." The "seven *times*" implies *duration* or *continuation* of punishment. But the word also conveys the meaning of *"sevenfold,"* or seven times greater *intensity* of punishment—as a punishment that is sevenfold more intense. In this sense, the meaning would be the same as in Daniel 3:19, where King Nebuchadnezzar, in a rage, commanded that the furnace into which Daniel's three friends were to be thrown should be made seven times hotter.

Now understand the "seven *times*"—or seven prophetic "times." For this *is* a prophecy. In prophecy, a *"time"* is a prophetic 360-day year. And, during Israel's punishment, each *day* represented a *year* being fulfilled.

This "day-for-a-year principle" is explained in two other passages dealing with the *duration* of Israel's punishment. One of these we have already covered. God punished that generation of Israelites Moses had led out of Egypt by *withholding* from them entry into the promised land FORTY YEARS. That promised land was a beginning *part* of the birthright. God punished them on the principle of a YEAR for every DAY—forty *years'* DURATION of punishment for the 40 *days* of transgression.

Ezekiel's "Day for a Year"

In order to impress on the prophet Ezekiel the *seriousness* of Israel's years of rebellion against God's rule and God's laws which would *cause* great blessings, God imposed this very principle on him—but it was enacted in reverse.

The *sins* of the house of Israel had continued from their rejection of God as King for 390 years. Naturally God could not expect this prophet, in a human lifetime, to undergo the bearing of these years of sin on the basis of each *day* of sinning being borne by him for a *year*.

That would have required 2,000 lifetimes. So God reversed the actual application of the principle. Ezekiel was required to bear Israel's sins a *day* for each *year* they had sinned. But it still was the "day-for-a-year principle"!

Ezekiel was told to lie on his left side, in an imaginary siege against Jerusalem, pictured on a tile before him. "Lie thou also upon thy left side, and lay the iniquity of the house of Israel upon it: according to the number of the days that thou shalt lie upon it thou shalt bear their iniquity. For I have laid upon thee *the years* of their iniquity, according to the number of the *days*, three hundred and ninety days: so shalt thou bear the iniquity of the house of Israel. And when thou hast accomplished them, lie again on thy right side, and thou shalt bear the iniquity of the house of Judah forty days: I have appointed thee *each day for a year*" (Ezek. 4:4-6). It is mentioned further in verse 9.

But in the other application of the "day-for-a-year principle," previously explained, where it applied also to *a duration* of punishment put on THE PEOPLE, the punishment was to be borne by them on the basis of a year of punishment for each *day*. Also in this case, the punishment was the number of *years* during which a promised blessing was withheld.

Now when we come to the expression "then I will punish you *seven times* more for your sins" in Leviticus 26, it is evident both by its manner of wording in the sentence and by the fact of actual fulfillment that it was speaking of a DURATION of seven prophetic "*times*," or YEARS. And on this "year-for-a-day principle," it becomes seven 360-day years—a total of 2520 *days*. And when each *day* is a *year* of punishment—in this case, as in Numbers 14:34, a withholding of a promised blessing—the punishment becomes the withdrawing of and

153

withholding the promised blessings for 2520 years! For that is precisely what did happen!

What is a "Time"?

But now did you notice I said that a prophetic *"time"* is a 360-day year? Why not a year of 365¼ days? Why not a solar year?

In ancient biblical times, a year was figured on a basis of twelve 30-day months. Previous to the time, in Moses' day, when God gave His people the sacred calendar, the 30-day month was used.

Notice Genesis 7:11: "In the six hundredth year of Noah's life, in the second month, the seventeenth day of the month, the same day were all the fountains of the great deep broken up, and the windows of heaven were opened." Now verse 24: "And the waters prevailed upon the earth an hundred and fifty days."

Next, Genesis 8:3-4: "And the waters returned from off the earth continually: and after the end of the hundred and fifty days the waters were abated. And the ark rested in the seventh month, on the seventeenth day of the month, upon the mountains of Ararat."

So notice—the flood started on the 17th day of the second month. At the end of 150 days, the ark rested on Mount Ararat, on the 17th day of the 7th month. That was five months to the day. Five 30-day months are precisely 150 days. So months, then, were 30-day months!

We find it definitely figured this way in both Daniel and Revelation. In Revelation 12:6, a prophecy of an event which in actual history did last 1260 solar years is spoken of as "a thousand two hundred and threescore days." So here, again, a prophetic *day* was a *year* in fulfillment. In Revelation 13:5 (referring to a different *event* but the same amount of time) this same period of 1260 *days* being fulfilled in 1260 solar years is spoken of as "forty and two months." Now 42 calendar months, according to the calendar now in use, would not be 1260 days, but 1276 days—and, if a leap year occurred, 1277. Or, if the extra *half*-year happened to be the *last* half of the year, it would be 1280 or 1281 days. But the 42 months of Revelation 13:5 is the same amount of time as the 1260 days of Revelation 12:6. So the 42 months were 30-day months.

The same amount of days is spoken of in still different language in Revelation 12:14 as "a time, and times, and half a time." The "time" is one prophetic year; the "times" is two more prophetic years; and the whole expression is 3½ prophetic "*times*," which is a literal 1260 *days*—or 3½ years of thirty-day months. Seven of these "times" then would be 2520 days—and on a day-for-a-year basis, 2520 years!

Then in Daniel 12:7 the same expression "time, times, and an half [time]" is mentioned.

Enough space is being taken here to make this concept plain, clear, understandable. For it is basic to several key prophecies.

A prophetic "*time*," then, is a 360-day year—or a plain 360 days. And during those years of Israel's punishment, as made plain by combining Leviticus 26:18 with Ezekiel 4:4-6, Numbers 14:34, and Revelation 13:5 and 12:6, each *day* of a prophetic "time" was one *year* in fulfillment. In Leviticus 26:18, and in Revelation 12:6 and 13:5, this meaning is verified and PROVED by the fact that the prophecy was fulfilled in precisely the time indicated.

Birthright Withheld 2520 Years

Now back again to the pivotal prophecy of Leviticus 26.

These Israelites had not listened to God—had not qualified to become recipients of the fabulous, overwhelming birthright national blessing. They had broken especially the two *test commandments* emphasized in verses 1 and 2 of this chapter. God had punished them in the manner He had said He would, as described in verses 14-17.

Now God said, as quoted before, "And if ye will not yet *for all this*"—all He had punished them with, described in verses 14-17—"hearken unto me, then I will punish you *seven times* more for your sins."

Because of the manner in which this warning is worded, compared with the manner of wording where the *"seven times"* is again mentioned—and because the birthright *actually was withheld* PRECISELY 2520 years—it is certain that the meaning of the *"seven times"* in verse 18 is a DURATION of seven 360-day YEARS, each *day* being *a year* in fulfillment—total: 2520 actual YEARS! And the very enforcing of the "day-for-a-year principle" also implies a multiplied *intensity* of the punishment.

Actually, they had sinned the 390 years mentioned in Ezekiel's prophecy (Ezek. 4:4-5). Even from the time they rejected God as their national King, God allowed them to remain in the promised land those additional 390 years! During all these years God continued to send prophets to warn and plead with them. Had they repented and turned back to God and His ways, they still could have received the richest national blessing of all history. But they would not. Rather, they increased in sins!

So finally God took completely away from them— for a duration of 2520 years—this opportunity to reap such vast material prosperity and power.

Israel Becomes Lost

Finally God *drove them out of the promised land!*

All these 390 years of national sin (Ezek. 4:5), of rejecting Him and His ways, God continued to deal with

156

them. He kept contact with them. He sent His prophets to them. At any time during these years of their rebellion, they could have repented, turned to God, and received this vast national status.

But now, at last, God drove them out of His land! He "removed them out of his sight" (II Kings 17:18).

Again it is repeated (verse 23), He "removed Israel out of his sight, as he had said by all his servants the prophets. So was Israel carried away out of their own land to Assyria unto this day."

From that time, God sent no prophets to them. He gave them no more chance to receive the greatest national blessing of all history—until the end of the 2520 years! He hid, as it were, His face from them! He removed them out of His sight. He pleaded no longer with them. They had not qualified for nor deserved His blessings! Now He left them a slave people, to shift for themselves. He left them to their own devices!

They had rejected even the identifying sign by which they were to be known and recognized as God's people Israel. So now they soon lost even their identity! No longer were they known by the world as God's people. No longer did they call themselves God's people.

They became lost! The "LOST TEN TRIBES." Lost in name. Lost in identity. Lost spiritually! They had lost their tremendous birthright—for a duration of many generations! In due time, as a second and third generation came along, they *lost* even their Hebrew language! They regarded themselves as Gentiles! The world supposed they were Gentiles!

Apostles to Britain?

Generations later, Jesus of Nazareth, well knowing where they had migrated, sent His twelve original apos-

157

tles to *make* known to them His precious gospel of God's Kingdom—God's government! It was the apostle Paul who was sent to the Gentiles.

Did you never wonder *why*, after Acts 15, we read no more of the twelve apostles? Except for a trip by Peter to Babylon, they had gone to "lost" Israel!

Regarding the original apostles, the Bible says: "These twelve Jesus sent forth, and commanded them, saying, Go NOT into the way of the Gentiles, and into any city of the Samaritans [Gentiles] enter ye not: But go rather to the LOST sheep of the house of Israel" (Matt. 10:5-6). Yes! The lost Ten Tribes.

But Jesus never begged, urged, pleaded with anyone to "get saved!" Nor did His apostles! That is a modern Protestant method. They merely proclaimed the truth, leaving it to every hearer to make his own decision whether to act on it.

Yes, the British Isles heard Christ's gospel! But they accepted, instead, the idolatry of the Druids, pagan worship, and the counterfeit "Christianity" of the Roman Babylonian mystery religion, and even spawned the devil's religion of the evolutionary concept.

Birthright Conferred at Last!

But when that 2520-year withholding of the birthright had expired, God was faithful to His unconditional PROMISE to Abraham! Not because of any British or American goodness, superiority, or worthiness, but because of God's faithfulness to His promise, beginning in 1800 these two birthright peoples *suddenly* burst forth as the greatest world powers in all history!

This national wealth and power came not because our peoples in any manner finally qualified for it. They never did! But consider:

The very fact of a withholding of the birthright

158

from them for a definite duration in itself implies a conferring of it at the end of the 2520 years. And remember, God had promised this birthright to the descendants of Abraham unconditionally because of Abraham's faithfulness and obedience (Gen. 26:5). God was bound by His promise to confer this stupendous national blessing regardless of the righteousness or wickedness of the descendants. But God had not bound Himself to bestow it upon any one particular generation.

Thus God was able to offer it conditionally to Old Testament Israel in and after Moses' day. The people of those generations could have had it upon compliance with the *conditions!* Denying it to those particular generations—withholding it for 2520 long years, even—did not violate God's unconditional PROMISE to Abraham.

But the very *fact* of a withholding for the definite duration of 2520 years implies the direct conferring of that national blessing on expiration of that definite period of withholding—*regardless* of any further qualifying or deserving on the part of the people. This must be so because of God's faithfulness to His UNCONDITIONAL PROMISE to Abraham.

So—beginning A.D. 1800-1803, after 2520 years— God did cause the birthright nations—and them *only*— to become *suddenly* the recipients of such national wealth, greatness and power as no nation or empire ever before had acquired! Together they—the British and Americans, descendants of only *one* original tribe, Joseph—came into possession of more than two-thirds— almost three-fourths—of all the cultivated resources and wealth of the whole world!

It sounds incredible! All other nations combined shared between them only little more than a fourth of the world's wealth. And that includes the nations descended from other tribes of Israel. It includes such

159

nations as Germany, Italy, Russia, China—all other nations on the whole earth.

The most amazing fact of all history is this sudden skyrocketing from virtual obscurity of two nations to the most fabulous wealth and economic power ever possessed by any people. Britain became GREAT Britain—a gigantic, stupendously wealthy commonwealth of nations—the United States, the greatest nation of history.

More amazing still are the unbelievably shocking facts of the present—of how—and WHY—we are *losing* it faster than it came!

WHY? The incredible facts, the reasons, and what's now ahead will follow!

11

Why Israel Lost Identity

THE MYSTERY IS NOW REVEALED! Not only the answer to *what happened* to the "LOST TEN TRIBES"— but also WHY they so completely *lost* their identity!

The main vanguard of the Israelites—the northern kingdom—who bore the national name "Kingdom of ISRAEL"—became a nation *lost* in all history.

So far as historic records are concerned, the earth might as well have opened her mouth and swallowed them.

History does record their captivity by Assyria, 721-718 B.C. They were removed from their cities, towns and farms in their northern part of Palestine, taken as slaves to Assyria, on the southern shores of the Caspian Sea. But by 604-585 B.C., when the southern kingdom of JUDAH was taken captive by Nebuchadnezzar of Babylon,

161

the Assyrians had migrated northwest—and the ten-tribed Israelites with them!

Utterly Lost

They were utterly GONE! They were lost from view! How far northwest they proceeded, or where they finally settled, comes to a blank page in history.

How do historians and theologians explain this?

Not *knowing* the true answer, they explain it erroneously. They *assume*, in error, that *all* Israelites were Jews, and that the thirteen million Jews in the world today constitute the entire population of Israelites remaining alive at this time. Some theologians falsely claim that all of the ten tribes who went into Assyrian captivity in 721-718 B.C. returned to Jerusalem with the Jews who returned to build the Temple there seventy years after Judah's captivity, 604-585 B.C. But that is total error. Only *part* of Judah went back. And those who returned were *all* of the three tribes of Judah, Benjamin and Levi. Check the genealogies in Ezra and Nehemiah.

The Jews are supposed to be Israel—and *all* of Israel—*because* they *never lost their identity!* There is a reason why the Jews did *not* lose their identity, while the house of ISRAEL *did!*

God had given them a very special everlasting COVENANT containing a SIGN of IDENTITY.

The Special Covenant of Identity

It is not generally known or recognized that the Eternal made with His people, while still at Mt. Sinai, a separate, special, eternally binding COVENANT, providing for a SIGN of IDENTITY.

At this juncture, it must be pointed out that these people Israel were the *only* people on earth with whom God then dealt personally as HIS PEOPLE.

Remember, Adam and Eve had rejected the symbolic tree that represented God's Holy Spirit, and a Father-and-son relationship with Him. Their descendants, cut off from God, strayed so far from His ways that by the time of Noah the earth was filled with corruption and violence.

After the Flood, within two generations the world as a whole was following the apostate ways of Nimrod (Gen. 10:8-12; 11:1-9), and his mother-wife founded the apostate pagan religion that has engulfed and deceived the world ever since. This apostate religious system, started by Semiramis, flowed into all nations. In its perversions of truth, it evolved into different *varieties* and appeared under different national *names* in different nations. But it was the same basic system of apostasy. It cut the world off from God! And it grips a deceived world TODAY—in its various forms, called by the names of various religions.

God selected these children of Israel because of the OBEDIENCE of Abraham, Isaac and Jacob. While they were in servitude and slavery He called them as HIS people, to whom HIS TRUTH—His true religion and way of life and intended DESTINY for mankind—should be revealed.

God's TRUTH and God's WAY revealed to these Israelites is simply God's TRUTH and His WAY for all peoples in all times and ages! Israel, had they followed God's ways, was intended to be a living EXAMPLE to all nations.

Jesus came, not to do away with God's TRUTH or God's WAY, not to bring a new religion, but to reveal additional truth about the coming Kingdom of God and how we may be born into it.

True, Old Testament Israel was given certain sacrificial rites and rituals which served merely as *a re-*

163

minder of sin (Heb. 10:1-4; 9:10), only as a temporary *substitute* for Christ—*until* He should come. When the reality came, the substitute was dropped. But God's TRUTH and WAY remain eternally! Therefore God was revealing to Israel what HIS WAY is for all people of all time—including TODAY!

This special identifying COVENANT, then, ordained FOREVER, applies to all Christians today—to all who are reconciled to God as HIS PEOPLE!

This special eternally binding COVENANT is found in Exodus 31:12-17. It has to do with one of those two *test commandments*, which, we saw in the last chapter, Israel was driven out and deprived of the birthright for violating.

The Identifying Sign

"And the LORD spake unto Moses, saying, Speak thou also unto the children of Israel, saying, Verily my sabbaths ye shall keep . . ." (Ex. 31:12-13).

Notice *which* day is "the Lord's day." The Eternal calls the Sabbaths "*my* sabbaths." The Sabbaths are His—they did not belong to Israel—they are not *our* days, but the Lord's. They are not "the Jewish Sabbaths" or "the Gentile Sabbaths." The Sabbath is a space of time. That time, whenever it arrives, is *not ours*, but God's.

And it applies the same to us today as to our forefathers then. If we appropriate it for ourselves—for our own use, whether work, pleasure, or whatever—we are stealing that time from God!

Notice again! He said: "My sabbaths ye *shall keep.*" In Exodus 20:8 He commanded us to "keep it [the Sabbath] HOLY"—God *made* it HOLY TIME and commanded us to *keep* it holy—not to profane what is holy to God.

BABYLONIAN MOTHERS bowing before Nimrod, high priest of the sun god, present their babies to be purified by being sacrificed in fire. Nimrod founded an apostate pagan religious system that has engulfed and deceived the world.

Now study this special covenant a little further: " . . . for it is a sign between me and you throughout your generations; that ye may know that I am the LORD that doth sanctify you" (Ex. 31:13). What *tremendous* meaning is packed in that portion of this sentence! Yet most people read right past it, failing to get the vital TRUTH it contains!

Notice! Here is the purpose of the Sabbath: " . . . *for it is a* SIGN. . . ." What is a *sign*?

You walk down a main street in the business section of a city. Everywhere you see *signs* identifying stores, offices, factories. If you want to know what a *sign* is, just turn to the word in the Yellow Pages (the classified business listings of your telephone directory). You will

165

find such names as "Jones Neon Sign Company" or "Smith Brothers Signs." If you call one of them on the telephone and ask, "What do you make or sell?" he will tell you that they make signs for business firms, institutions, or professional individuals to hang in front of their places of business. The sign *identifies* whose establishment, institution or office is inside.

It Identifies

A sign is a badge, symbol, or token of identity. You see the sign, "A. B. Brown, Furniture and Furnishings." The sign identifies the *owner*. It tells you what kind of business he owns. Webster's dictionary defines a sign thus: "A publicly displayed notice on a building, office, etc. to advertise the business there transacted, or the name of the person or firm conducting it. Something indicating the existence of a thing; a token." And, of course, there are the special technical meanings in mathematics, medicine, astronomy.

The word which Moses wrote in the Hebrew language which is translated "sign" is *'ôwth*, and the Hebrew-English dictionary defines it as "signal, as a flag, beacon, monument, evidence, etc.—mark, miracle, sign, token." A flag identifies a nation. A beacon is a signal to announce the existence of something warned about. A token is a visible sign; something that serves as an identifying signal to make something known, as a white flag is a token of surrender.

God commanded His people to keep His Sabbath as a *sign*. It is a sign between God's people and God: " . . . a sign between me and you," the commandment says. It is a badge or token of IDENTITY. It advertises, or announces, or proclaims certain identifying knowledge. But WHAT KNOWLEDGE? God answers: " . . . that ye may *know* that I am the Lord that doth sanctify you."

166

Who Is God?

Note those words carefully! It is the *sign* that IDENTIFIES to them who is their God! It is the sign by which we may *know* that He is the Lord! It identifies God!

But doesn't everybody know who God is? Absolutely not! This whole world is deceived—so says your Bible.

This world has a god—a false god—Satan the devil! He pretends to be "an angel of light" (II Cor. 11:14). He has his religious organizations—his churches. Not all are Buddhist, Shintoist, Taoist, Confucianist. Many have appropriated the very name "Christian," but their ministers, says your Bible, actually are Satan's ministers: "And no marvel; for Satan himself is transformed into an angel of light. Therefore it is no great thing if his ministers also be transformed as the ministers of righteousness" (II Cor. 11:14-15).

But do they actually call themselves the ministers of CHRIST? Read the verse just before the two just quoted—verse 13: "For such are false apostles, deceitful workers, transforming themselves into the apostles of Christ." Yes, Satan is the great counterfeiter. He palms himself off as GOD. He is called, in your Bible, the *god of this world* (II Cor. 4:4). He palms off his ministers as the ministers of CHRIST—and they accuse the *true* ministers of Christ of being "false apostles" to divert suspicion from themselves!

Does this world's "Christianity" *really* know the TRUE GOD? It is *deceived* into believing it does, and a deceived world may be sincere in that false belief. One's *god* is the one, or the thing, whom he serves and obeys. But the true GOD is the One whom we *should obey.*

This world is not taught to OBEY GOD! Its false "Christianity" teaches that God's law is "done away." It actually puts human conscience, actuated by Satan's false teaching, in place of God's law! It does not teach, as did Christ, that we must actually *live* by every word of GOD—all of the BIBLE! It OBEYS Satan by *sinning*! Satan, therefore, is this world's god!

The Purpose of the Sabbath

God gave man His Sabbath for the purpose of keeping mankind in the true knowledge and true worship of the true GOD. But *how* does the Sabbath identify God—how does it point to the *true* God, rather than the false? Does not Sunday do just as well? Positively not!

Notice verse 17 of this special Sabbath covenant: "It is a sign between me and the children of Israel for ever: for in six days the LORD made heaven and earth, and on the seventh day he rested, and was refreshed" (Ex. 31:17).

It was on *the seventh* day of that creation week that He rested from the work of creation. Not Sunday, the first day of the week. Only *the seventh* day of the week points back to CREATION.

How does *that* identify who GOD is?

If you believe anyone else or anything else is God, I will *prove* that my God is the true God, because whatever else you may think is God was made or created by the true God. He who created and made *everything else* is GREATER than whatever He made—superior to anything else that could be called god.

CREATION is the *proof* of God—of His existence. It—the act of creating—*identifies* Him!

So God took the most enduring, lasting, imperishable thing man can know—a recurring space of time—the *only* day that is a memorial of the act of creating. He took the *only day* which points, constantly, every *seventh* day of the week, to God's resting on the seventh

168

day of creation week from CREATING; which points to the existence of the Almighty, All-Powerful, All-Ruling God—the Creator!

And God set that particular day apart from others as His day—God made that particular day sacred and holy to HIM—designating it as the *very* day on which HE commands His people to assemble for WORSHIP—the day man is commanded to REST from his own work and physical pleasure—and to be refreshed by assembling with other obedient worshipers in spiritual fellowship!

No other day is a memorial and reminder of CRE-ATION. True, Satan has deceived a deluded world into supposing Christ's resurrection occurred on Sunday morning at sunrise—the very time which has always been the time of pagan SUN worship. But this supposition is not true! Write for our free booklet about the resurrection (*The Resurrection Was Not on Sunday!*). You will be amazed! Also write for our special free booklet on Easter (*The Plain Truth About Easter*). They are shocking eye-openers—and the truth you can verify and prove at your public library.

The resurrection of Christ actually occurred on *the Sabbath*, not on Sunday! And, further, *nowhere* in the Bible does God tell us to celebrate the day of Christ's resurrection! That is a pagan custom of MEN, on apostate man's authority alone—contrary to the commands of GOD!

Identifies People of God

So here we find a GREAT PURPOSE in the Sabbath. It identifies God! The very day which God set aside for assembly and worship points as a memorial to whom we are to worship—the CREATOR-RULER of all that is!

But *that is not all!* The Sabbath also was given as a sign which identifies WHO are the PEOPLE of God and who

169

are not! Notice! Not only does this special covenant say, " . . . that ye may know that I am the LORD . . . " but read the remainder of that sentence: " . . . that ye may know that I am the Lord that doth sanctify *you*" (Ex. 31:13).

Notice the tremendous MEANING of that!

What does the word "sanctify" mean? It means "to set apart for holy use or purpose." On the seventh day of the very creation week, the Eternal *sanctified*—that is, HE SET APART for HOLY use—the Sabbath day. But now we see that God says it is a sign that He, the Eternal, also sanctifies—sets apart from other people as *His*, FOR HIS HOLY PURPOSE—those who are His people.

In Old Testament times His people were the people of ISRAEL. In New Testament times, His people are those of God's own Church—the truly converted, spirit-begotten CHRISTIANS!

But HOW does the Sabbath set them apart—separate them—from those who are *not* God's own true people?

Well, if you have begun to keep God's Sabbath holy, as He commands, you have found the answer already, by actual experience. If you haven't, just start keeping God's Sabbath holy as He commands you—and you'll soon learn that you are automatically *set apart* from all other people! The world, people you *know*—some of your family and relatives, business associates, or contacts—*they* will set you apart!

The Sabbath is God's SIGN, which identifies not only GOD as CREATOR-RULER, but it also identifies those who are truly HIS people!

But HOW?

Definition of God

Let me give you still another definition of GOD. Although the only wise and true God is the Great Creator-

Ruler of the universe, there are many false or counter-feit gods. Satan palms himself off to the deceived as God—and indeed the Bible plainly calls him the god of this world. Idols were worshiped as gods—and still are, today, even in so-called "Christian" churches. Whoever, or whatever, you *serve* and *obey* is your god!

The very word "Lord" *means* ruler, master, boss—the one you obey! Jesus exclaimed: "And why call ye me, Lord, Lord, and *do not* the things which I say?" (Luke 6:46.) If they did not OBEY Him, then He was *not* their Lord! So WHY did they *call* Him LORD, when He was *not* their Lord?

Then again, Jesus said: "Not every one that saith unto me, Lord, Lord, shall enter into the kingdom of heaven; but he that doeth the will of my Father which is in heaven" (Matt. 7:21). Only they who OBEY God can be His children and enter His Kingdom! Your God is the one you OBEY!

Notice again: "Know ye not, that to whom ye yield yourselves servants to OBEY, his servants ye are to whom ye OBEY?" (Rom. 6:16.)

Regarding idols as false and counterfeit gods, the second commandment says: "Thou shalt not bow down thyself to them, *nor serve them* [that is, OBEY them]: for I the Eternal thy God am a jealous God, visiting the iniquity [disobedience] of the fathers upon the children unto the third and fourth generation of them that hate me; and shewing mercy unto thousands of them that love me, and keep my commandments" (Ex. 20:5-6).

The Real Test Commandment

How significant! The Sabbath command is the ONLY one of the ten which is a SIGN identifying WHO are the real and true Christians today! It is the real test command!

A man may be honest and upright in his dealings

with others—he may have a reputation of not lying or stealing. But that does not IDENTIFY him—set him apart—especially as a *Christian!*

Many non-Christians honor their parents—at least so far as other people know. Many are regarded by others as truthful, true to husband or wife; many do not swear or use profanity; and most are not murderers—in the eyes of others.

But their supposed conformity to *these* commandments does not stamp them as *different*—as being God's people! Actually, few keep even *these* commandments *in the spirit*, but that is not obvious to the world. But it *is* VERY obvious to the world when one keeps God's Sabbath!

That's why few do! People don't want to be identified as being apart from the world—as belonging to GOD, *apart from* the world! People want to be identified, in the eyes of others, as belonging to the world—but feel ashamed to be identified, in the eyes of friends, business contacts, relatives, as belonging to God.

The people of the world are willing to acknowledge the other nine commandments—but the Sabbath command is the one they positively REBEL against! It is THE ONE that is the crucial test of obedience! It IDENTIFIES those who have *surrendered* their wills to God—who OBEY God, regardless of persecution or cost!

Oh, it sets you apart, all right! What a SIGN!

It identifies the TRUE GOD on the very DAY He set apart for assembly and worship. It identifies the REAL people of God! It identifies those who keep the Sabbath as being God's people—*to the world*, that is! Actually, few Jews really *keep* the Sabbath HOLY! It may not identify them to God as His people, *spiritually!* But they *do* at least acknowledge that particular day! And even though in God's sight they profane it, it identifies them to the world!

172

*Ezekiel prophesied:
"As I was among
the captives by the
river of Chebar . . .
the heavens were
opened, and I saw
visions of God."*

(Ezekiel 1:1)

God's SIGN is one you accept voluntarily—of your own volition, or not at all. But the "beast" (symbol of the coming resurrected, so-called Holy Roman Empire in Europe) has a MARK, which is soon going to be BRANDED ON, by physical FORCE! And it has something to do with "buying or selling"—trading, business, earning a living, having a job (Rev. 13:16-17; Rev. 13 and 17). Yes, this is the TEST COMMAND—the one on which YOUR VERY SALVATION and ETERNITY DEPEND!

I have said that God made the Sabbath a separate, eternal, and perpetual covenant entirely separate and apart from what we term "the Old Covenant" made at Mt. Sinai. How, then, is it a COVENANT?

173

But Is It a Covenant?

Let's define the word "covenant." Webster defines a covenant as: "An agreement between persons or parties. A solemn compact." A covenant is a contract, or agreement, by which one party promises certain rewards or payments in return for certain stipulated performance by the other party.

The Old Covenant between God and the children of Israel made at Mt. Sinai *imposed* upon the people certain terms and conditions to be performed: obedience to the Ten Commandments. It *promised* the reward of making Israel a nation "ABOVE all people." The promises were purely national and material, for *this* world. The NEW Covenant is founded on BETTER PROMISES (Heb. 8:6), which consist of an "ETERNAL inheritance" (Heb. 9:15).

Once a covenant is signed, sealed, or ratified—confirmed—it cannot be added to (Gal. 3:15). Anything appearing beneath the signature is not legally any part of the covenant. You read of the actual *making* of the Old Covenant and sealing it *with blood* in Exodus 24:6-8. And notice (verse 8), it concludes with the words "the covenant, which the LORD *hath made* with you." It was then already made—completed.

We do not come to the making of this special eternal Sabbath covenant until seven chapters *later*. It is, therefore, NO PART OF the Old Covenant!

But, again, *is it* a COVENANT?

The wording in your Bible *says* it is! Notice Exodus 31:16: "Wherefore the children of Israel shall keep the sabbath, to observe the sabbath throughout their generations, for *a perpetual covenant.*"

"Perpetual" means continuous and unbroken. But was it to last FOREVER? Read the following verse: "It is a SIGN between me and the children of Israel *for ever.*"

174

Now what is the condition to be performed? The keeping holy of the Sabbath! "It is HOLY unto you," says God (verse 14). And what is the reward promised upon performance of the condition? It is not only a SIGN, but also a compact or COVENANT "between me and you," says God, "that ye may know that I am the LORD *that doth sanctify you.*"

There it is! God promises TO SANCTIFY THEM—He will set them apart as HOLY—as HIS HOLY PEOPLE! Can you ask for a BIGGER promise?

Yes, it is a COVENANT! It is a *separate*, totally different covenant. Even if one tries to argue that the Old Covenant is "abolished" and that therefore the Ten Commandments are abolished, he cannot argue that *this* covenant was to last only until the cross. The covenant is binding "throughout your generations" (verse 13); "a perpetual covenant" (verse 16) and "for ever" (verse 17).

Sign for Israel Only?

"Yes," says the rebellious one who would argue his way out of obedience, "but it is between God and the children of ISRAEL. It is throughout Israel's generations; it is between God and the ISRAELITES forever."

Oh—then you admit it is binding FOREVER on ISRAELITES—and throughout *their* generations? There are TWO answers to that argument that will condemn you, if you so argue, to the LAKE OF FIRE!

1) No one can deny that this absolutely BINDS the people of Israel to keep the Sabbath FOREVER, and throughout their generations perpetually. Their generations are still going on. Therefore it is binding on them today.

Also you have to admit that salvation and Christianity are open to Jews and all Israelites. The gospel "is

175

the power of God UNTO SALVATION to every one that believeth; TO THE JEW FIRST, and also to the Greek" (Rom. 1:16).

So then the Jew can be a converted CHRISTIAN! Indeed, the Church at the beginning was nearly altogether Jewish! So the JEW, even though a Christian in God's CHURCH, is BOUND to keep God's Sabbath as a perpetual covenant, throughout his generations, FOREVER!

Now, does God have TWO KINDS of Christians? Is it SIN for a Jewish Christian to break the Sabbath, and sin for all others to KEEP it? Must Jewish Christians assemble on the Sabbath, and those of other nationalities on Sunday? Didn't Jesus say a house divided against itself would fall?

Are there TWO KINDS of Christians? Read Galatians 3:28-29: "There is neither Jew nor Greek, there is neither bond nor free, there is neither male nor female: for ye are ALL ONE IN CHRIST JESUS. And if ye [Gentiles] be Christ's, then are ye Abraham's seed, and heirs according to the promise."

So, since the Sabbath is BINDING TODAY on the Jewish part of God's Church, and there is no difference —we are all ONE in Christ—it is also binding on Gentiles!

We Are Israel

2) But there is another answer to this argument: The peoples of the United States, the British Commonwealth nations, and the nations of northwestern Europe are, in fact, the peoples of the TEN TRIBES of the HOUSE OF ISRAEL. The Jewish people are the house of JUDAH.

But IF the Sabbath is God's SIGN to identify His people Israel, then why don't our nations keep it today?

The answer to that question is the answer to another: Why are the Ten Tribes of the HOUSE OF ISRAEL called "the LOST Ten Tribes"? And why do our nations think they are Gentiles? Why don't they KNOW their true identity?

Ah, now we have a staggering, startling, surprising truth to reveal! Here's a dumbfounding truth, far stranger than fiction!

Here are FACTS, hidden for centuries, more intriguing than a mystery novel! Why is the Sabbath called, disrespectfully, sneeringly, "the *Jewish* Sabbath"? WHY does the world think all Israelites are Jews, and that the Jews are ALL of the Israelites?

Here's an astonishing surprise to those who have believed that! The Jews are only a small minority of the Israelites.

Israel Lost Sign

Nowhere in all the Bible are any of the ten-tribed nation of Israel called Jews. That name—JEWS—applies only to the kingdom of JUDAH. Jews are Israelites, truly—but only *part* of the Israelites are Jews!

Almost immediately on being made a king, Jeroboam became afraid that, when his people journeyed to Jerusalem to attend the annual festivals, they would see and desire Rehoboam again for their king. He took swift action to protect his own position.

The tribe of Levi composed the priesthood. They were the leaders—the best educated. The Levites, living off the tithes, had enjoyed incomes two or three times larger than the other tribes. With one swift stroke, Jeroboam demoted the Levites, set the lowest and most ignorant of people to be the priests. He could control them! Thus he would control the religion, like Gentile kings had always done. Thereupon many, if not most, of the Levites went back into the kingdom of JUDAH—and became known as JEWS.

So immediately Jeroboam set up two great idols for his people to worship. He ordered the fall festivals to be observed in the *eighth* month, at a place of *his* choosing north of Palestine—instead of in the seventh month, and at Jerusalem as GOD ordered (I Kings 12:28-32). Also Jeroboam changed the Sabbath day from the seventh to the eighth—that is, to the day *following* the seventh day, which, of course, was actually the *first* day of the week. Thus he set the day for worship to coincide with the pagan DAY OF THE SUN, now called Sunday!

Through the rule of 19 kings and seven successive dynasties, the ten-tribed house of Israel continued in the basic twin sins of Jeroboam: idolatry and Sabbath-breaking. Several of the kings added other evil and sinful practices.

But in 721-718 B.C., God caused the house of Israel to be invaded and conquered by the kingdom of Assyria. These Israelites were removed from their farms and their cities and taken to Assyria on the southern shores of the Caspian Sea *as slaves*. But the house of JUDAH— the Jews, a separate and different nation—were not invaded until 604 B.C.

Two or three generations after the captivity of Israel, however, the Chaldeans rose to WORLD POWER, forming the first WORLD-ruling empire. Under Nebuchadnezzar the Chaldeans (Babylon) invaded JUDAH (604-585 B.C.).

The Assyrians—before 604 B.C.—left their land north of Babylon and migrated northwest—through the lands that are now Georgia, the Ukraine, Poland, and into the land that is called GERMANY today. Today the descendants of those Assyrians are known to us as the GERMAN people.

The people of ten-tribed Israel also migrated northwest. Though the Assyrians had taken Israel into captivity, the Israelites did not remain as slaves of the Assyrians in Europe. They continued on a little further—into
Western Europe, the Scandinavian peninsula, and the
British Isles!

Now why did they come to be known as the "LOST
Ten Tribes"? They had lost their national identifying
sign!

King Jeroboam had changed their day of worship
from the seventh to the first day of the week—the day of
the SUN—Sunday! All succeeding kings followed this
practice, as well as idolatry!

As long as they remained in the LAND of Israel and
called themselves "the KINGDOM OF ISRAEL" their identity was known. But in Assyria they were no longer a
nation with their own government and their own king.
They were mere slaves. They took up the language of the
Assyrians as succeeding generations grew up. They lost
the Hebrew language as biblical prophecy said they
would. They lost all national identity.

After several generations, the tribe of Joseph, divided into the *two* tribes of Ephraim and Manasseh,
came to call themselves British. They retained a few
Hebrew earmarks. *Berith* or *b'rith* in Hebrew means
"covenant," and *ish* means "man." Thus, in Hebrew,
British means "covenant man," which, truly, they
are.

The tribe of Reuben settled in the country that is
France today. They had lost their national identity. But
the French have the very characteristics of their ances-
tor, Reuben. Today, through our free booklet in the
French language revealing this ancestry and national
identity, thousands of French people are beginning to
learn their own true identity.

THE UNITED STATES AND BRITAIN IN PROPHECY

The TEN TRIBES, known as the house of ISRAEL, lost their identifying tag—God's Sabbath.

That is why they lost their national identity!

Why Jews Are Recognized

But JUDAH kept the Sabbath! They did not continue long to keep it holy, or to keep it *God's way*—but they did recognize it, as they do today, as the day of rest they acknowledge and observe. Result? All the world looks on them as the chosen people of God! The world thinks they are ISRAEL—not merely Judah!

The Jews' identity has not been lost! And since their identity as racial descendants from ancient Israel is known—and that of the far more numerous "LOST TEN TRIBES" is *not* known—the world supposes that the Jews are ISRAEL, instead of JUDAH. The Jewish people believe it themselves! And so, here again, the whole world is deceived, even as to the true identity of who really *are* the chosen birthright people of God!

Yes, the Sabbath, God's day—the true Lord's day—is, after all, the day for our people doubly: first, because it is for ALL people of GOD, even Gentile-born people who are now Christ's; secondly, because racially, even by fleshly birth, it is God's day which He gave our own forefathers and commanded to keep holy FOR-EVER!

Why Israel Made Slaves

Do you know WHY the kingdom of Israel was invaded by Assyria, conquered, removed from their land as slaves in 721-718 B.C.? Do you know WHY the JEWS (kingdom of Judah) were later taken captive and scattered over the world? Both houses of Israel were sent into national punishment and banishment from Palestine because they broke God's Sabbath!

Does it make any difference? It certainly made a lot of difference to GOD! And He says He has not changed— He is the *same* yesterday, today, and forever! (Heb. 13:8.)

First, see why the Jews were invaded, conquered by Nebuchadnezzar and taken into Babylonian captivity during the years 604-585 B.C.

Seventy years after that captivity, according to Jeremiah's prophecy (Jer. 29:10), many of the Jews returned to Palestine to rebuild the Temple and restore the worship there. The prophet Nehemiah tells why they had been driven into captive slavery 70 years before: "In those days saw I in Judah some treading wine presses on the sabbath, and bringing in sheaves, and lading asses; as also wine, grapes, and figs, and all manner of burdens, which they brought into Jerusalem *on the sabbath day*: and I testified against them in the day wherein they sold victuals. . . . Then I contended with the nobles of Judah, and said unto them, What evil thing is this that ye do, and profane the sabbath day? Did not your fathers thus, and did not our God bring all this evil upon us, and upon this city? Yet ye bring more wrath upon Israel by profaning the sabbath" (Neh. 13:15-18).

There it is in plain language! Sabbath-breaking was a prime cause of Judah's captivity! It was so *important* to GOD that He punished His own chosen people with this most severe national punishment—defeat in war, being taken from their land and made SLAVES in a foreign land! SIN is defined by GOD as the transgression of His LAW (I John 3:4). His LAW says: "Remember the sabbath day, to keep it holy. . . . the seventh day is the sabbath of the LORD thy GOD." To work on the Sabbath,

181

to defile it by your own pleasure seeking, doing business, etc. is A MAJOR SIN, punishable by ETERNAL DEATH!

Jews Were Warned

The Jews were without excuse. They had been warned by the prophets. Notice the warning through Jeremiah: "Thus saith the Eternal; Take heed to yourselves, and bear no burden on the sabbath day . . . neither do ye any work, but hallow ye the sabbath day, as I commanded your fathers. . . . But if ye will not hearken unto me to hallow the sabbath day, and not to bear a burden, even entering in at the gates of Jerusalem on the sabbath day; then will I kindle a fire in the gates thereof, and it shall devour the palaces of Jerusalem, and it shall not be quenched" (Jer. 17:21-22, 27).

That was the warning. The Jews did not heed it. Now see what happened!

"Now in the fifth month, in the tenth day of the month, which was the nineteenth year of Nebuchadrezzar king of Babylon, came Nebuzar-adan, captain of the guard [today we would call him general of the armies, or field marshal], which served the king of Babylon, into Jerusalem, and burned the house of the Eternal, and the king's house; and all the houses of Jerusalem, and all the houses of the great men, burned he with fire" (Jer. 52:12-13).

When God *warns*, the punishment is SURE!

Why Israel Defeated

Now see what happened to the *other* nation of Israelites, the kingdom of Israel, 117 years before Judah's captivity.

God had laid down the choice to these people in the days of Moses, long before they were divided into two nations. This was fully covered in the previous chapter, regarding Leviticus 26. Now see what God said about it through the prophet Ezekiel.

182

Ezekiel was given a message from God to the HOUSE OF ISRAEL (not Judah—the Jews). Ezekiel was among the Jewish captives after *their* captivity, which occurred more than a hundred years after Israel's captivity. By that time the Assyrians had long since left their land on the southern shores of the Caspian Sea and migrated northwest, finally settling in the land today called Germany.

The people of the house of Israel also migrated northwest across Europe. But they did not stop in Germany. They continued on farther west and north—into Western Europe—France, Belgium, Holland, the Scandinavian countries, and the British Isles—where they are to this day, except for the tribe of Manasseh, which much later migrated to North America and became the United States.

The prophet Ezekiel was commissioned to go from where he was, among the Jews, to the HOUSE OF ISRAEL. "Go speak unto the HOUSE OF ISRAEL," said God (Ezek. 3:1), and again: "Go, get thee unto the house of Israel" (verse 4).

But Ezekiel never took that message to the lost house of Israel. He couldn't. He was a slave among the Jews.

Yet he is taking it to them, today, by means of having written it in his book in the Bible—and by the fact that it is being taken to those very people today by *The Plain Truth* and *The World Tomorrow* broadcast!

It is a prophecy! It is a message for our peoples today! You are reading it NOW! God help you to heed!

Prophecy to Us, Today

Speaking first of ancient Israel, God says, in Ezekiel 20: "Wherefore I caused them to go forth out of the land of

183

Egypt, and brought them into the wilderness. And I gave them *my* statutes, and shewed them *my* judgments, which if a man do, he shall even live in them. Moreover also I gave them *my* sabbaths, *to be a sign* between me and them, that they might know that I am the LORD that sanctify them" (verses 10-12).

Notice, this passage repeats the exact wording of the forever-binding Sabbath covenant of Exodus 31:12-17! Now continue: "But the house of Israel rebelled against me in the wilderness: they walked not in *my* statutes, and they despised *my* judgments . . . and *my* sabbaths they greatly polluted" (verse 13).

Then God pleaded with their children, a generation later: "But I said unto their children in the wilderness, Walk ye not in the statutes of your fathers, neither observe *their* judgments, nor defile yourselves with *their* idols: *I* am the Eternal your God; walk in *my* statutes, and keep *my* judgments, and do them; and hallow *my* sabbaths; and they shall be a sign between me and you, that ye may know that I am the Eternal your God" (verses 18-20).

The entire emphasis here is differentiating between God's statutes, judgments and sabbaths on the one hand, and *their fathers'* different sabbaths, statutes and judgments. They were observing a *different day* from God's Sabbath! They had already turned to the pagans' day, today called SUNday—the day of the SUN and SUN worship!

"Notwithstanding the children rebelled against me," continued God, through the prophet Ezekiel. " . . . They polluted MY sabbaths" (verse 21).

So what did God finally do—generations later?

He scattered them, in national captivity and slavery (verse 23). But WHY?

"Because they had not executed *my* judgments, but

184

had despised *my* statutes, and had polluted *my* sabbaths, and their eyes were after *their fathers'* idols"
(verse 24). That's why! Did it make any DIFFERENCE?

But now continue on in this amazing prophecy!
Notice the prophecy FOR US, TODAY!

Speaking of a time, sometime soon, in OUR time,
God says to OUR peoples: "As I live, saith the Lord Eternal, surely with a mighty hand, and with a stretched out
arm, and with FURY poured out, will I RULE OVER YOU"
(verse 33).

The expression "fury poured out" refers to the SEV-
EN LAST PLAGUES, at the very time of the second coming
of Christ (compare Rev. 16:1). The time when Christ will
RULE over us is at and after His second coming. So this,
then, is a PROPHECY for OUR TIME!

Every prophecy in the Bible showing *where* our
people (Israel) will be, at the second coming of Christ
and the coming great exodus back to Palestine, pictures
them *in captivity and slavery* ONCE AGAIN.

Continue the prophecy: "And I will bring you out
from the people, and will gather you out of the countries
wherein ye are scattered . . . with FURY POURED OUT. And
I will bring you into the wilderness of the people [COM-
ING EXODUS—Jer. 23:7-8], and there will I plead with you
FACE TO FACE" (verses 34-35).

Notice it! This is the Word speaking—CHRIST! He
will then be on earth again in person! And then He is
going to plead with our people FACE TO FACE.

It's time to awake to the *imminency* and the stark
SERIOUSNESS of this!

Perhaps only one lone voice is warning you! But
God used one lone voice to warn the world in Noah's
day; one lone voice in Elijah's day; one lone voice in the
day of John the Baptist; and after John the Baptist was
put in prison, one voice in the person of Christ Himself!

185

If you rely on the majority of sinning people, you will suffer their penalties with them!

Notice how He will plead!

"Like as I pleaded with your fathers in the wilderness of the land of Egypt, so will I plead with YOU, saith the Lord Eternal. . . . And I will purge out from among you the rebels, and them that transgress against me . . . and ye shall know that I am the Lord" (verses 36-38).

How did He plead with them? He pleaded: "Hallow MY sabbaths, instead of your fathers', so that you may KNOW that I am the LORD." And those of us who do go into Palestine shall KNOW HE is the LORD.

How shall we know?

By His Sabbath sign!

Read verses 42-44 in your own Bible! He says our people, when they are no longer rebellious and who will then be keeping His Sabbath, shall remember their ways in which they were defiled and shall LOATHE themselves for their Sabbath-breaking! This is pretty strong teaching! It is the Word of God speaking to YOU!

12

The Birthright— at Its Zenith— and Now!

OW GREAT, HOW POWERFUL, AND
how wealthy did the British and
American people become? And
what is suddenly happening to us now? Why has Britain
already *lost* most of her colonies—her possessions—her
resources, wealth, power and influence in the world?
Why is Britain no longer considered Great Britain—a
GREAT world power?

Why is the United States now discredited, despised, hated throughout so much of the world? Why
could we not *win* the Korean War? Why couldn't the
United States whip little North Vietnam?

First, realize just how great—how rich and
powerful—the American and British people did become.

People are prone to take their status—and that of
their country—for granted. Few realize what unprecedented affluence our countries enjoyed. We judge all
things by *comparison*. The average Briton, Australian

or Canadian has never traveled through the illiterate, poverty-stricken, disease-infested backward areas of China, India, the Middle East or black Africa. He has not observed the squalor, the stench, the poverty and wretchedness in which the largest part of mankind lives.

Nor has the average American visited those vast underprivileged areas, nor even the countries of Europe—prosperous compared to the teeming illiterate masses, yet poor by comparison to American standards. No, our people generally have not realized. Nor have they been grateful. Nor have they given God thanks, nor accepted the responsibility that accompanies their lavish blessings.

Few realize that every desired, prized possession imposes with it the obligation of responsibility for its use. Does the eight-year-old boy who is given a shiny new bicycle by his parents feel a consciousness for the responsibility imposed on him—unless the fact is impressed on him by his parents—for the *care* of it, and the carefulness with which he must ride it to avoid injuring himself or others?

When God lavished on our peoples such wealth and power and economic possession as no peoples have ever before enjoyed, did we appreciate what we had or feel the commensurate sense of RESPONSIBILITY for its wise and proper use?

WE DID NOT! We didn't even recognize HOW GREAT was our blessing, let alone feel a sense of obligation for our custodianship before our Maker! Just HOW GREAT, then, was this birthright blessing?

The Birthright Wealth

Read again the prophetic promises of Genesis 22:17.

To Abraham God said: "That in blessing I will bless

thee, and in multiplying I will multiply thy seed as the stars of the heaven, and as the sand which is upon the sea shore; and thy seed shall possess the gate of his enemies."

And again, the inspired prophetic parting blessing upon Rebekah, leaving her family to become the wife of Isaac: "And they blessed Rebekah, and said unto her, Thou art our sister, be thou the mother of thousands of millions, and let thy seed possess the gate of those which hate them" (Gen. 24:60).

Earlier we quoted the correct Fenton translation: " . . . and your race shall possess the gates [plural] of its enemies." As explained there, the "gates" of enemy nations are the strategic SEA GATES of entrance to or exit from these nations. Although all wealth comes from the ground, prosperity and affluence on a national scale always have come also by industry and COMMERCE. And commerce between nations has been transacted almost altogether by the SEA-LANES of the world—by SHIPS, and, within a continent, by railroads.

How significant, then, that Robert Fulton operated the first steamboat in 1803—precisely when Britain and America suddenly began to MULTIPLY in national wealth! And also that it was the nineteenth century that saw the development of the railroads!

As explained before, since the birthright pertains to NATIONS, the "GATE" of our enemies would be such passes as Gibraltar, Suez, Singapore, the Panama Canal, etc.

Britain and America came into possession of every such major "gate" in this world! So we MUST be modern Israel. World War II hinged on these "gates." They had become not only strategic passes, but the world's greatest fortifications. But today, we have lost most of them, most recently, the Panama Canal—and it appears that soon Gibraltar, too, will be lost. Why?

189

Notice Genesis 39:2, 23: "The Eternal was with Joseph, and he was a PROSPEROUS man. . . . the Eternal was with him, and that which he did, the Eternal made it to PROSPER." And God *did* prosper Joseph's descendants, Britain and America, with the fabulous birthright promised Joseph's sons!

Consider Moses' dying prophetic blessing, foretelling what would happen to each of the tribes in these latter days.

"And of Joseph he said, Blessed of the Lord be his land, for the precious things of heaven, for the dew, and for the deep that coucheth beneath, and for the precious fruits brought forth by the sun, and for the precious things put forth by the moon, and for the chief things of the ancient mountains, and for the precious things of the lasting hills, and for the precious things of the earth and fulness thereof . . . let the blessing come upon the head of Joseph [Ephraim and Manasseh both]. . . . His glory is like the firstling [firstborn—birthright holder] of his *bullock*, and his horns are like *the horns of unicorns* [Great Britain's national seal today]: with them he shall push the people together to the ends of the earth: and they are the ten thousands of Ephraim, and they are the thousands of Manasseh" (Deut. 33:13-17).

Whoever is Ephraim and Manasseh today must have been in possession of the earth's choicest agricultural, mineral, and other wealth—the great gold and silver mines; iron, oil, and coal; timber and other resources.

What nations fulfill these prophecies? Why, *only* Great Britain and America!

More than half of all tillable, cultivatable, temperate-zone lands of this earth came after A.D. 1800 into the possession of our two great powers alone! The rich agricultural lands of the Mississippi Valley; the vast wheat and grain fields of the Midwest, of Canada and Australia; the great forest lands of the Pacific Northwest and many other parts of the world; the gold fields of South Africa, Australia, Alaska and the United States; the great coal mines of the United States and British Isles; the natural waterfalls and means of power and consequent prosperous industrial and manufacturing districts of England and the eastern United States; the choicest fruit lands of our Pacific Coast and Florida. What other nations *combined* ever possessed such material wealth?

And nearly all this wealth came to us after A.D. 1800!

The Actual Statistics

Just to what extent has Almighty God fulfilled His promises *in us* to the descendants of Joseph in these latter years since A.D. 1800—promises of "the precious fruits brought forth by the sun . . . the chief things of the ancient mountains . . . and the precious things of the earth"?

Said Charles M. Schwab, steel magnate, before the Massachusetts Bankers Association, January 5, 1921: "Our United States has been endowed by God with everything to make it and keep it the foremost industrial and commercial nation of the world."

World petroleum output in 1950 was almost 3,800 million barrels. Of this total the United States *alone* produced more than one-half—nearly 52%. Together, the British Commonwealth and the United States produced 60% of the crude petroleum, not including our vast foreign investments. But by 1966—the fateful year in which the British Colonial Office in London closed its doors, marking the official death of the British Empire—that 60% of all the world's crude petroleum output had been reduced to 32%.

191

Britain and America mined 1½ times as much coal as all other nations combined. But by 1966 our portion had shrunk to less than one-third of the world production—30.9%!

Together, the British Commonwealth and America produced, in 1950, three-fourths of the world's steel—the United States alone producing almost 60% or 105,200,000 short tons in 1951. We produced 1⅓ times as much pig iron as all other nations combined.

By 1966, this basic index of wealth had skidded down to one-third (33.6%) of steel production and only 17.8% (one-sixth) of the pig iron.

We possessed nearly 95% of the world's nickel (chiefly from Canada); 80% of the world's aluminum; 75% of the zinc. But where did we rate in 1966? Only 3.6% of the world's nickel; 40.2% of its aluminum (aluminium); 12.4% of its zinc.

In 1950, the British Commonwealth completely dominated the production of chromite (from South Africa). Together Britain and America produced two-thirds of the world's rubber, and dominated the world's copper, lead, tin, bauxite and other precious metal outputs. But by 1966, we produced only 2.3% of the world's chromite, 23.4% of its copper, 9.9% of its lead, no tin, and 6.3% of its bauxite.

The British Commonwealth produced two-thirds of the world's gold—about £266,000,000 ($642 million) in 1950—while the United States had three times as much gold reserve as the total for the rest of the world. But by 1966 the U.S. gold supply had been drained so much that the dollar was in serious jeopardy.

We produced and utilized two-thirds of the world's output of electricity—the United States producing 283 thousand million kilowatt-hours in 1948, and the United Kingdom and Canada outstripping Russia, Germany

192

and France combined. But by 1966 we produced only 20.1%!

Great Britain and the United States *did* possess well over half of the world's merchant fleet tonnage. But by 1966 the figure was only 32.5%. The British Isles constructed more vessels than any other place on earth. But less than two decades later two or three Gentile nations had already outstripped Britain and America. In 1950, we also possessed about one-half of the world's railroad mileage. By 1966 our combined railway freight shipping was only 26% of the world total.

Whereas the United States alone once produced 73% of the automobiles, by 1966 the U.S. combined with the U.K. produced 55%—44% from the U.S. alone. Japan, Germany, France, and Italy are making huge gains.

How Did We Get It?

How did we come into possession of all this vast wealth of the earth? Did we acquire it through our own human wisdom, foresight, energy, ability and power?

Let Abraham Lincoln answer: "We *find ourselves* in the peaceful possession of the fairest portion of the earth, as regards fertility of soil, extent of territory, and salubrity of climate. . . . We . . . *find ourselves* the legal inheritors of these fundamental blessings. *We toiled not in the acquirement or the establishment of them.*"

Again, in his proclamation of April 30, 1863, for a nationwide day of fasting and prayer, this great president said: "It is the duty of nations, as well as of men, to own their dependence upon the overruling power of God . . . and to recognize the sublime truth, announced in the Holy Scriptures and proven by all history, that those nations *only* are blessed whose God is the Lord . . . . We have been the recipients of the choicest

193

blessings of heaven. We have been preserved, these many years, in peace and prosperity. We have grown in numbers, wealth and power *as no other nation ever has grown;* BUT WE HAVE FORGOTTEN GOD! We have forgotten the gracious Hand which preserved us in peace, and multiplied and enriched and strengthened us; and we have vainly imagined, in the deceitfulness of our hearts, that these blessings were produced by some superior wisdom and virtue of our own."

And because Lincoln saw a nation who had forgotten God—a nation drunk with a success not due to its own efforts—a nation taking all the credit and glory to itself, this great president called upon the nation for a day of fasting and prayer to confess this national sin before God. The fate of the nation hung in the balance when he issued that proclamation. But God heard and answered that great national prayer offensive—and the nation was then preserved!

But today the threat to our fate is a thousand times more seriously hanging in the balance. And today we do not have a president or a prime minister with the vision, understanding and courage to bring our nations to their knees!

Abraham Lincoln *knew* these great material blessings had not been earned, but had been *given* to our people by the God of Abraham, Isaac, and of Israel.

And we should face the facts today and *know* that we were given all this vast unprecedented material wealth because God *promised* it, unconditionally, to Abraham. And He promised it to Abraham because Abraham obeyed God, kept God's laws and commandments.

The birthright blessing was *denied* our forefathers after Moses' day because they REFUSED to live by God's laws.

194

And today God warns us, through many prophecies in Jeremiah, Ezekiel, Isaiah, Micah, and many others, that unless we of this generation REPENT of our sins, and turn to Him with fasting, and with weeping, and earnest PRAYER, He will destroy our cities, all our fortresses, with the foreign sword; that He will punish us at the hand of a CRUEL ONE; that we shall be invaded, defeated, reduced to SLAVES! GOD HELP US TO HEED THAT WARNING!

In conclusion, we ask: If *we* are not national Israel—the so-called "lost" Ten Tribes—prosperous Joseph-Israel—birthright Israel—actual inheritors of the birthright blessings which were to be bestowed beginning A.D. 1803, then who else can be? No other nation or combination of nations possessed these blessings of the birthright—for we held more than two-thirds—nearly three-fourths—of all the raw materials, resources, and wealth of this entire round earth, and all other nations combined shared among them only a small part.

Do you know of *stronger proof* of the divine inspiration of the Holy Bible as the revealed Word of the living God? Could mortal men have written, without divine inspiration, those prophecies we have considered in this book; made those PROMISES to Joseph-Israel; and, after a lapse of 2520 years, beginning the exact years of 1800-1803, have had power to bring them about in fulfillment? These are no small or trifling promises. They involve possession of the great wealth and vast natural resources of the whole earth.

Present these facts as a challenge to your atheistic and agnostic friends. Ask them to answer, if they can, whether any but the power of the Eternal Creator Himself could have made and had committed to writing such promises thousands of years ago, and, at precisely the promised time thousands of years later, brought about their fulfillment!

How any American—any English-speaking inheritor of God's choicest material blessings—can, in the face of such stupendous, overwhelming fulfillment of prophecy—such awe-inspiring demonstration of the power and might and faithfulness of Almighty God—accept and partake of these blessings, and then carelessly ignore God's WARNING that our sins today are INCREASING, or fail to get to his knees before the great Almighty, repent, and INTERCEDE in heartrending PRAYER for all Israelite nations, and HELP in every way he can to warn our people now of their impending PERIL, seems impossible to conceive.

13

And Now What? The Prophecies For The Immediate Future

THE BIRTHRIGHT, ONCE WE RE-
ceived it, was stupendous, AWE-
SOME—unequaled among nations or
empires! But what have our peoples done with that awesome blessing?

They were still ISRAELITES, even though they themselves knew it not! They were still rebellious, "stiff-
necked," stubborn!

Once the British peoples and the Americans—the
"lost" Israelites now supposing they are Gentiles—
found themselves basking in the pleasant sunshine of
such wealth and power, they were less willing than their
ancient forefathers to yield to their GOD and HIS WAYS.
They felt no need of Him, now! It seems few ever turn to
God until they find themselves in desperate need or
trouble.

But after God had withheld the birthright 2520

years, and then, when our peoples deserved *nothing* from God, He *suddenly* bestowed on us national blessings unparalleled in history—the unconditional promise to Abraham was kept! *No longer* is God obligated by His promise to *continue* our undeserving peoples in world prestige, wealth and greatness. Once we had been *given* such unrivaled position, it was up to us whether we should keep it.

So now back to Leviticus 26. We had previously covered verses 1 through 18. God said that IF, for all these previous punishments, the Israelites would not listen to and obey Him, He would punish them the duration of 2520 years. Then what?

If, after that 2520 years of *withholding* the birthright, our people—*with* the birthright—still rebel, God continues, *verse 19:* "And I will break the pride of your power; and I will make your heaven as iron, and your earth as brass." God has already begun that!

We Had Pride in Our Power!

God could not speak about breaking the pride of our national POWER until after that birthright power had been bestowed! He put our nations in the position of possessing the greatest national power any nation or empire ever possessed. We had great *pride* in that national power—in our national prestige.

I remember hearing President Theodore Roosevelt tell of HIS PRIDE in that power—and how he used it when he was president. The Germans were sending a battleship steaming toward Manila Bay, threatening to take over the Philippines. The Philippines were then a United States possession. President Roosevelt sent the kaiser a terse note demanding that the German warship be immediately withdrawn.

"The kaiser didn't know, then, that *I meant it!*"

snapped Mr. Roosevelt. "So I sent another note. Only, I didn't send this second note to the kaiser. I sent it to Admiral Dewey, in command of the United States Pacific fleet. It ordered the entire fleet to steam full speed toward the German battleship, and if it did not turn around and go back, to SINK IT!" said Mr. Roosevelt with emphatic *force!* In those days, before World War I, we had *pride* in our national power!

... *But We Lost It!*

Today even little nations dare to insult, trample on, or burn the United States flag—and the United States, still having power, does no more than issue a weak protest! What's *happened* to the PRIDE of our power?

We have already LOST IT! God said, "I will break the pride of your power!" And HE DID!

Other prophecies reveal we are to have soon such drought and famine that disease epidemics will follow, taking millions of lives. When our heaven is as iron, our earth as brass, we will realize rain does not come down from iron, and an earth hard as brass is not getting rain, not yielding food!

Verse 20: "And your strength shall be spent in vain: for your land shall not yield her increase, neither shall the trees of the land yield their fruits."

But will America and Britain *heed?* They never have!

Then what? After all that, THEN WHAT?

Verse 21: "And if ye walk contrary unto me, and will not hearken unto me; I will bring *seven times more plagues* upon you according to your sins."

There again, as in verse 18, is that Hebrew word *shibah.* Actually, in the Hebrew in which Moses wrote, there are not the two Hebrew words, one meaning "seven" and the other "times." There is just the one word, *shibah.*

THE UNITED STATES AND BRITAIN IN PROPHECY

As explained previously, the word is defined as "seven times," and also as "sevenfold." The "seven times" conveys *duration* of punishment. The "sevenfold" meaning of the same word conveys *intensity* of punishment.

Now More Intense Punishment

Because of its use and construction in the sentence, and because of what actually happened, it is certain that in verse 18 this Hebrew word *shibah* refers to DURATION of punishment—seven prophetic times, which, during this punishment, was an actual 2520 YEARS!

But also, because of the very *different* sentence structure and because there cannot now be *another* 2520-year WITHHOLDING of what has now been bestowed, it is just as certain that the *shibah* in verse 21 refers to a sevenfold INTENSITY of punishment. Notice, the wording in verse 21 is entirely different from verse 18. This time it is not worded "seven times more for your sins," but "seven times more PLAGUES." The expression "seven times" in verse 21 is descriptive of PLAGUES to be brought on them.

So now, if twentieth-century Ephraim and Manasseh—Britain and America—refuse to turn to God in obedience—refuse to live the way that *causes*, retains, and increases blessings, God will punish them in a manner far more INTENSE—and even strip entirely from them this colossal, unprecedented national blessing— returning them to captivity and slavery—as continuing verses of this prophecy show.

Do you think so great a fall could not come to so great powers as Britain and America? Do you say, "It

---

THE FLAG OF THE UNITED STATES is set ablaze by anti-U.S. demonstrators. American power and leadership has steadily declined to where the United States is called a "paper tiger."

can't happen HERE?" Do you think the GREAT GOD who was able to GIVE them such unprecedented world leadership and power and wealth is not able to take it away from them and throw them, like their ancient forefathers, back into SLAVERY?

You need to OPEN YOUR EYES to the *fact* that Britain's sun *already has* SET! You need to WAKE UP to the *fact* that the United States, even still possessing unmatched POWER, is *afraid*—fears—to *use it*, just as God said: "I will break the PRIDE of your POWER"; that the United States has *stopped winning wars*—that America was *unable*, with all its vast power, to conquer little North Vietnam! The United States is fast riding to the GREATEST FALL that ever befell any nation!

The handwriting is on the wall!

You need, now, to UNDERSTAND the *remainder* of this prophecy of Leviticus 26—and also of Deuteronomy 28—and the many other prophecies relating to them and events soon to VIOLENTLY affect YOUR life!

You need to look at the prophecies of Jesus, of Jeremiah, of Isaiah, and others describing how much more intense is to be the punishment God is going to lay on the British and American people.

For MANY prophecies warn us of a CERTAINTY that it will be trouble such as NEVER happened to any nation or people!

Knowing our identity—knowing *how* the British and American peoples are identified in the prophecies— you need now to become AWARE of what is said about us in Isaiah, Jeremiah, Ezekiel, Daniel, Joel, Hosea, Amos, and the other prophecies—*what* JESUS *foretold*—as well as in these prophecies written by Moses!

And you need, also, to know why a just and loving God is going to punish His chosen people—people He *chose* for a glorious PURPOSE they have refused to perform.

The very *fact* of punishment implies CORRECTION. We need to understand that correction is applied to correct WRONG WAYS harmful to *us*—to turn us around into RIGHT WAYS that will *cause* desired blessings! Understand! God *punishes* every son He *loves* (Heb. 12:6).

Understand also human nature! Human nature wants to *be* good—to consider itself and *be* considered *good*, while it wants only to *do* evil. It wants the good *result*. But it wants to receive the *good* while it sows the evil. It somehow fails to grasp the truth that *as* we sow, so also shall we reap! It's all a matter of CAUSE and EFFECT!

God's punishment only reflects God's LOVE—turning us from *causing* evil results to the way that brings *happy* results! God is now about to STOP US from bringing colossal evils on ourselves! God is not angry because we are harming HIM—but because we are harming *ourselves*—whom God *loves!*

Punishment Is Correction

The prophecies do not stop with revealing the unprecedented multiplied *intensity* of punishment already beginning to descend upon America and Britain. The prophecies record also the RESULT of that intensified punishment. The *result* will be a corrected people. The result will be an eye-opening realization of what we have done to ourselves. The supreme punishment will teach us, at last, our lesson! The punishment will *break* our spirit of REBELLION! It will lift us up from the cesspool of rottenness and evil into which we have sunk. It will teach us the way to glorious peace, prosperity, abundant well-being!

On beyond the frightful national calamities now descending upon us will come a BLESSING inconceivably greater than the national material birthright we have possessed.

We have to learn that material goods are not the SOURCE of happiness. I have often mentioned the many rich men I have known—men whose bank balances were full—but their lives were empty! Material prosperity is indeed desirable—but it is not the source of happiness.

After all, real happiness is a *spiritual* commodity! The birthright was only one of TWO major promises God made to Abraham. The sceptre promise involved not only a dynasty of human kings. It need not have included them at all—had the Israelites retained and been obedient to GOD as their King. The sceptre pointed primarily to CHRIST and spiritual salvation through Him.

Our peoples have basic lessons yet to learn. The TRUE VALUES are spiritual. Actually, God's law is a spiritual law. It involves physical acts—but it is based on *spiritual* principles. And it requires God's Holy Spirit dwelling in the mind to fulfill!

PUNISHMENT implies CORRECTION. Correction means a change of course. It means REPENTANCE—and repentance means *turning around* and going the OTHER WAY!

Now, before I give you these sensational prophecies, understand WHY national punishment must come, and *who needs* the correction! ONLY those who are sowing EVIL *need* it—who are transgressing God's right WAYS—God's law! Those, and only those, who are bringing on themselves the evils that result from transgression.

And UNDERSTAND THIS: Although the NATIONS as a whole are to be put through this unprecedented punishment, yet those *individuals* who yield to accept God's

204

correction *without the punishment* shall be protected from it! No one need suffer this intense tribulation!

Sevenfold More Plagues

Now notice again what is laid down in Leviticus 26.

After the national birthright had been withheld 2520 years and *then* bestowed; *after* God *gave* our peoples that national POWER, and has now, because of our national rebellion against His laws, *broken* the pride of our power; *after* He shall have punished us with unprecedented DROUGHT and epidemics of disease in its wake, then IF the British and Americans still continue in their evil ways—still refuse to repent and turn to their God—He warns: "... I will bring seven times more PLAGUES upon you according to your sins." Read that in the Revised Standard Version: "... I will bring more plagues upon you, sevenfold as many as your sins" (verse 21).

What people do not seem to realize is that SIN does bring upon the sinner the *consequences* of sin—the plagues of suffering. The Bible defines sin as the transgression of God's law (I John 3:4), and the law of God is a *spiritual* law (Rom. 7:14).

Let's understand this! I have said that *money* is not the source of happiness. Money can buy only material things or services. But there must be the *spiritual* content, as well as the physical, to happiness. Material things *alone* do not provide satisfying happiness. God's law is a *spiritual* law. In other words, it is THE WAY to peace, happiness, abundant well-being. Going that way is what God supplied to CAUSE real happiness.

Conversely, then, can we not see that transgressing that way is to cause *un*happiness, pain and suffering, emptiness, heartaches, fears and worries, frustrations? All these *evils* are *caused* by transgressing God's law.

The sinner is really *plagued* with these evils he brings on himself.

Now study again that 21st verse of Leviticus 26. Punishment *is* CORRECTION. To *teach* us the lesson we have failed to learn by experience, God is going to plague our peoples SEVENFOLD more than our sins already *have* plagued us—sevenfold *more* punishment than we have brought on ourselves!

Or, as the Authorized Version says, "seven times more plagues upon you *according to your sins.*" Sevenfold INTENSITY of punishment—OF CORRECTION!

Slavery Once Again

Notice now verses 23-25 (RSV): "And if by this discipline you are not turned to me, but walk contrary to me, then I also will walk contrary to you, and I myself will smite you sevenfold for your sins. And I will bring a sword upon you . . . and you shall be delivered into the hand of the enemy."

SLAVERY once again!

Get the real meaning of this! Our SINS have brought punishment. This punishment we have brought on ourselves. If we still refuse to learn the lesson, and be corrected for our own good, God says, "I myself will smite you sevenfold." We have brought the consequences of SIN on ourselves—now God will Himself bring on us sevenfold more intense punishment—punishment that is CORRECTION!

Now read on to verse 33 (RSV): "And if in spite of this you will not hearken to me, but walk contrary to me, then I will walk contrary to you *in fury* [the seven last plagues—Rev. 15:1], and chastise you *myself* sevenfold for your sins. . . . And I will LAY YOUR CITIES WASTE. . . . And I will scatter you among the nations."

God is going to keep multiplying chastening—correction—upon our peoples *until* they *do* turn from their evil ways—until they turn *to* the ways that *cause* peace, happiness, prosperity, all the *good things!*

How UNTHINKABLE!—that our Maker shall have to *force* our peoples to be happy, to have peace, to be able to *enjoy* prosperity, to yield, to accept—our own choice—*eternal life* in abundant well-being and JOY for all eternity!

How UNBELIEVABLE!—that human nature, *desiring* these blessings, has insisted stubbornly in going the way that cuts them off and *causes* PUNISHMENT—CORREC-TION—and then refuses to *be* corrected until it is MULTI-PLIED in *intensity sevenfold!* Yes, sevenfold—three successive times!

How GREAT is our God—and WHAT LOVE for our peoples He expresses, in patiently tolerating and correcting us UNTIL we accept His boundless BLESSINGS!

14

What's Prophesied To Happen, Now— To America And Britain

JUST AS GOD HAS BESTOWED ON US such material blessings as *never before* came to any nations, now to correct us so we may enjoy such blessings, He is going to bring upon our peoples such national disaster as has *never before* struck any nation! Many prophecies describe this!

The Tremendous Prophecy of Micah

An important additional proof of modern Israel's identity is found in a fantastic, detailed and *most specific* prophecy found in Micah 5:7-15. It is speaking specifically about the "remnant" of Israel—modern Israel *today*—wherever it is. It describes the *wealth*, the beneficent dominance among nations, and then the coming *downfall* of the American and British Commonwealth peoples in detail!

Notice: "And the *remnant of Jacob* shall be in the midst of many people [nations] as a dew from the Lord, as the showers upon the grass, that tarrieth not for man, nor waiteth for the sons of men" (verse 7). Remember that dew and showers are *absolutely necessary* to agricultural productivity and are a symbol of national BLESSING and WEALTH from God.

Continue: "And the *remnant* of Jacob shall be among the Gentiles in the midst of many people as a lion among the beasts of the forest, as a young lion among the flocks of sheep: who, if he go through, both treadeth down, and teareth in pieces, and none can deliver" (verse 8).

Again, this symbolism describes the *last generation* of Israel as a GREAT POWER—as a lion among the other nations of the earth.

"Thine hand shall be lifted up upon thine adversaries, and all thine enemies shall be cut off" (verse 9). They WERE cut off from the beginning of God's birthright blessing on America and Britain starting about 1803, through the First World War, the Second World War, until the turning point of the Korean War at the end of 1950.

Since that time, however, these blessings are surely being *taken away*—and neither America nor Britain has come out on top in any major skirmish since that time!

So this prophecy shows that *at the very time* we were receiving God's blessings, we were a tremendous BLESSING to the other nations of the earth—for it is *our peoples* who have rescued the other nations of the world time and again through the Marshall Plan, the Point Four program, the Alliance for Progress, the hundreds of millions of bushels of wheat for India and other starving nations, etc. The Hoover Program saved up vast food supplies after World War I. It saved millions in *other* nations from starvation!

Anciently Joseph saved up the wheat and food and made it available to others. MODERN Joseph did also. *BUT*—we are stiff-necked and rebellious toward God and His law, while our ancient forefather Joseph served and obeyed God with a whole heart.

It is *our peoples* who have been like a "lion" among the other nations of the earth—*preserving* in two great world wars the peace of the world and stability for all human life on this planet!

Sudden Destruction

Yet, in this detailed prophecy, God says: "And it shall come to pass IN THAT DAY, saith the Lord, that I will cut off thy horses" ["war-horses," Moffatt translation]—tanks, ships, rockets—"out of the midst of thee, and I will destroy thy chariots: and I will *cut off the cities* [by hydrogen bombs?] of thy land, and throw down all thy strong holds" (verses 10-11).

God says He will do this! GOD determines the outcome of wars (Ps. 33:10-19).

How plain can you get? Here God identifies the GREAT peoples of the earth who are the most wealthy and beneficent, the most POWERFUL—yet *at the very time* their power reaches its zenith, He suddenly "breaks" the pride of their power (see Leviticus 26:19), *cuts off* their implements of war and destroys their cities! Why?

Because, as the prophet continues to explain, we have too much "witchcraft" and too many "soothsayers"—false ministers—in our lands who refuse to preach with authority the commandments and ways of the living God!

Therefore, God will punish and *destroy us—unless*

210

we repent—just before and leading up to the utter destruction to come *"upon the heathen"* (verse 15), which will take place at the very END of this age and at the second return of Jesus Christ as King of kings!

There is no other people that even remotely fulfills this great prophecy! But the American and British Commonwealth peoples fulfill it precisely!

As the "pride of our power" continues to be BROKEN, as the British continue to lose their foreign sea gates and possessions around the earth, as America signs away ownership of the Panama Canal—control over this vital sea gate—as our gold supply drains away from this nation, weather upsets increase, this focal prophecy alone represents giant PROOF as to where the modern "remnant" of the peoples of Israel resides today!

Punishment on All Nations!

It will now be made plain—from God's own warning prophecies—that this greatest multiplied *intensity* of corrective punishment will fall on Britain and America—including British peoples in Commonwealth countries. And it will strike them down *first!*

But they are not the only nations to suffer corrective disaster. God is Creator of all other nations, too! God is concerned about the people and races we have called "heathen." They, too, are human. They, too, are made in God's own likeness, with the potential of being molded into God's spiritual and character IMAGE! God sent the apostle Paul to Gentile nations!

All mankind has rebelled against, rejected, and turned from God and His ways! There can never be peace on earth until all nations will have been turned to God and His ways, ruled by His supreme government!

All mankind, right now, is caught in the vortex of the swiftly accelerating crisis marking the utter destruction of this world's man-built, Satan-inspired civilization.

Through Jeremiah God says: "A noise shall come even to the ends of the earth; for the Eternal hath a controversy with the nations, *he will plead with all flesh*"—how? Right now *The World Tomorrow* program carries His *peaceful* pleading worldwide, but the world, except for scattered individuals, does not heed *this* kind of "pleading." The next words tell HOW God is now about to plead: " . . . he will give them that are wicked to the sword, saith the Eternal. . . . Behold, EVIL shall go forth *from nation to nation*, and a great whirlwind shall be raised up from the coasts of the earth" (Jer. 25:31-32).

God will use a Nazi-Facist Europe to punish Britain-America. Then He will use the Communist hordes to wipe out the Roman Europe.

We are entering a time of world trouble—utter WORLD chaos! There is war, strife, violence in Asia, Africa, South America—as well as Europe and North America. The population explosion is a worldwide threat to human existence. Crime, violence, sickness, disease, inequality, poverty, filth, squalor, degeneration, suffering—these infest ALL nations!

But, as salvation is given *first* to Israel, so is corrective punishment!

Our Great Tribulation

Notice Jeremiah's prophecy:

"For thus saith the Eternal; We have heard a voice of trembling, of fear, and not of peace. Ask ye now, and see whether a man doth travail with child? Wherefore do I see every man with his hands on his loins, as a woman in travail, and all faces are turned into paleness? Alas! for that day is great, so that none is like it: it is even the time of Jacob's TROUBLE" (Jer. 30:5-7).

212

Remember—in passing on the birthright to the two sons of Joseph, Ephraim and Manasseh (Gen. 48:16), Jacob said, "Let MY NAME be named on them"—on Ephraim and Manasseh—who today are Britain and America. This tells ON WHOM this most terrible of national calamities is to fall—on Britain and America!

But now when is it to fall? Do not assume this is referring to anything that did happen to ancient Israel. Read right on—see WHEN this prophecy is to be fulfilled!

Continue in Jeremiah 30:7: " . . . it is even the time of JACOB's trouble; but he shall be saved out of it." (After he has learned his lesson *IN* it!) Continuing from RSV, "And it shall come to pass in that day, says the Eternal of hosts, that I will break the YOKE from off their neck [yoke of slavery], and I will burst their bonds, and strangers shall no more make servants of them. But they shall serve the Eternal their God *and* David their king, whom I will *raise up* for them." (David, at the time of the RESURRECTION—at the very time of Christ's COMING!)

So *the time* is just prior to Christ's COMING—coming *to liberate* our peoples—even as Moses liberated ancient Israel from Egyptian slavery.

Jesus Foretold It!

Other prophecies speak of this same time of national calamity greater than any before. The pivotal New Testament prophecy is that of Jesus on the Mount of Olives—recorded in Matthew 24, Mark 13, and Luke 21.

The apostles had asked Jesus privately WHEN His second coming would occur—and the END of *this* world and the beginning of the happy world tomorrow. Jesus said the SIGN by which we might know when this is very NEAR would be that His original gospel of the Kingdom of God would be preached in all the world as a witness to all nations (Matt. 24:14). But what else—just before His coming?

Jesus continued: "For then shall be GREAT TRIBULATION, such as was not since the beginning of the world to this time, no, nor ever shall be. And except those days should be shortened, there should no flesh be saved [alive]: but for the elect's sake those days shall be shortened" (Matt. 24:21-22).

Here is described the greatest time of TROUBLE—TRIBULATION—in all history, or ever to be. Jeremiah described it as "Jacob's trouble," so great "that none is like it."

Daniel described the same most severe trouble of all history. Speaking of a time now in our immediate future, Daniel foretold: "And at that time shall Michael stand up, the great prince [archangel] which standeth for the children of thy people: and there shall be a time of TROUBLE, such as never was since there was a nation even to that same time" (Dan. 12:1).

The same *most intense punishment* on Britain and America. And WHEN? Continue, same verse, " . . . and at that time thy people shall be delivered [from this enslaved trouble], every one that shall be found written in the book. And many of them that sleep [are dead] in the dust of the earth shall awake [RESURRECTION], some to everlasting life . . . " (verses 1-2).

The time is just before the RESURRECTION of the just, at Christ's coming. As Moses delivered the ancient Israelites from Egyptian slavery, so CHRIST is coming to deliver modern Britain and America from the now-impending *Babylonish* slavery. (See Deuteronomy 18:15; Acts 7:37; Jeremiah 23:5-8.)

Jeremiah described it as a "YOKE" on the necks of our peoples. WHOSE "YOKE" of slavery? Isaiah tells us!

214

In verse 1 of Isaiah 47 the prophetic message is addressed to the *daughter* of Babylon. *Not* the Babylon of ancient days. Not Nebuchadnezzar's Babylon of 600 years before Christ—but a DAUGHTER of that Babylon, now, in our twentieth century. In prophecy a woman, or a daughter, means a CHURCH—a religious organization.

This particular "lady" of this prophecy is pictured as a lewd harlot and "a lady of kingdoms." That is, a great CHURCH ruling over nations. This *same* modern "female" Babylon is pictured also in the 17th chapter of Revelation—there called a "great whore," sitting on or ruling over "many waters," which are interpreted in verse 15 as "peoples, and multitudes, and nations, and tongues." Her name is there given as "mystery, Babylon the great, the mother of harlots and abominations of the earth." In other words, the Babylonian mystery religion—the same religion of the ancient Babylon—but now grown GREAT and ruling over many nations of different languages.

Her KINGDOMS over which she ruled were called "The Holy Roman Empire" of A.D. 554 to 1814, briefly revived by Mussolini and SOON to have a last and final "resurrection" by a political-military union of ten nations in Europe (Rev. 17:8-14).

And the TIME of this "great whore" sitting astride the political-military "beast," they shall fight in war against the glorified CHRIST at His second coming (Rev. 17:14).

Now back to Isaiah 47. God says to this mistress of kingdoms: "I was wroth with my people [Israel—Britain-America], I have polluted mine inheritance, and given them *into thine hand* [in tortured slavery]: thou didst shew them no mercy; upon the ancient hast thou very heavily laid thy yoke" (verse 6).

That YOKE of SLAVERY without mercy is to be laid on

the U.S. and Britain by the coming united nations of Europe! It has started already, through the economic Common Market and the recently implemented EMS (European Monetary System). Its leaders talk continually of POLITICAL union—which means, also, military. So far they have been unable to bring about full political union. This will be made possible by the "good offices" of the Vatican, who alone can be the symbol of unity to which they can look. Two popes already have offered their "good offices" toward such union.

The prophecy does not literally say so, but in all probability, by present indications, the head of this new WORLD POWER will be in central Europe. And it will precipitate World War III. And this time it will be allowed to succeed!

Many of the ancient Assyrians migrated NORTHWEST from their ancient land south of the Caspian Sea—and settled in central Europe, just as the House of Israel migrated from the land of their captivity to the coastlands of northwest Europe. So when you read about Assyria in prophecies pertaining to NOW, they refer to central Europe!

So, history is to repeat! It was ancient Assyria which invaded the House of Israel, and carried them out of Samaria into the Assyrian's own land.

And where, today, are the ancient BABYLONIANS—the Chaldeans? They migrated west and settled in ITALY. Their religion was the Assyrian-Babylonian MYSTERY religion. It is going to come as a breathtaking, awesome, shocking surprise when the world learns that one Simon, the sorcerer of Samaria in the time of the original apostles, leader of the BABYLONIAN MYSTERY religion having the title of PATER or PETER, meaning PAPA, actually appropriated the NAME of *Christ* and the Christian principle of GRACE, which he turned into LICENSE, doing away

216

with GOD'S LAW (Jude 4) and started what is today called "Christianity." How astonished the world will be to discover that it is NOT, and never was, the outgrowth of the CHURCH OF GOD, founded by Jesus Christ and His apostles!

This knowledge will soon burst on an incredulous world as a BOMBSHELL! People will be SHOCKED to learn how they have been DECEIVED! When God's time comes, the "newsbomb" will be exploded!

What Is the Great Tribulation?

Now it becomes painfully clear! The Great Tribulation *is* this sevenfold intensity of corrective punishment which God is now soon going to lay on Britain-America!

Notice a few brief excerpts from Ezekiel's description of it!

"A third part of thee shall die with the pestilence, and with famine shall they be consumed in the midst of thee: and a third part shall fall by the sword round about thee; and I will scatter a third part [the remainder] into all the winds [slavery], and I will draw out a sword after them. THUS shall MINE ANGER be accomplished, and I will cause MY FURY [last PLAGUES] to rest upon them, and I will be comforted: and *they shall know* that I the Eternal have spoken it in my zeal, when I have accomplished my fury in them" (Ezek. 5:12-13).

Further: "In all your dwellingplaces the CITIES shall be laid waste" (Ezek. 6:6). This could never have happened until the hydrogen bomb! Cities laid completely WASTE. ALL of them—"in all your dwellingplaces."

Drought — Famine, First

Now let the prophet Joel add more.

Joel's prophecy was for the far, far future—verses

1-3 of chapter 1. Then he shows a plague of different kinds of locusts, devouring the fruits and food crops— stripping off bark from fruit trees. "He hath laid my vine waste, and barked my fig tree: he hath made it clean bare, and cast it away; the branches thereof are made white" (Joel 1:7).

Continue—now comes devastating DROUGHT: "The field is wasted, the land mourneth; for the corn is wasted: the new wine is dried up, the oil languish-eth. . . . because the harvest of the field is per-ished. . . . all the trees of the field, are withered: because joy is withered away from the sons of men" (verses 10-12). This is to happen just prior to the terrible plagues of "the DAY OF THE LORD" (verses 14-15).

Continue the prophecy: "The seed is rotten under their clods, the garners are laid desolate, the barns are broken down; for the corn is withered. How do the beasts groan! the herds of cattle are perplexed, because they have no pasture; yea, the flocks of sheep are made desolate. O LORD, to thee will I cry: for the fire [hot sun] hath devoured the pastures of the wilderness, and the flame hath burned all the trees of the field. The beasts of the field cry also unto thee: for the rivers of waters are dried up . . . " (verses 17-20).

Next—Military Invasion and Defeat!

Next in time order, beginning chapter 2, the alarm of WAR: "Blow ye the trumpet in Zion [alarm of WAR], and sound an alarm in my holy mountain: let all the inhabi-tants of the land *tremble:* for the DAY OF THE LORD cometh, for it is nigh at hand" (verse 1).

"Therefore also now, saith the Eternal, turn ye even to me with all your heart, and with fasting, and with weeping, and with mourning: And rend your heart, and not your garments, and turn unto the Eternal your God:

218

for he is gracious and merciful, slow to anger, and of great kindness, and repenteth him of the evil" (verses 12-13).

AT LAST!—Repentance in Tribulation!

Once God does add these repeated SEVENFOLD-INTENSITY of corrective punishments on our peoples—when they have had their wealth, prosperity, their land—the birthright and everything they possessed and set their hearts on TAKEN AWAY FROM THEM—AT LAST they will be humbled and will cry out to God for mercy and deliverance!

Right now GOD'S WARNING MESSAGE of this terrifying greatest trouble of history is being THUNDERED over *The World Tomorrow* program into ALL PARTS OF THE WORLD—*as a witness!* Some two and a half million are reading it in *The Plain Truth!*

We know only too well that the people as a whole will not heed! We are grateful that God is laying it on the hearts of a few thousand every year to LISTEN (hearken—to use biblical Authorized Version language) and to take it seriously—to REPENT and come to God through Jesus Christ as Savior.

Yes, a few thousand every year—thousands PRECIOUS beyond estimate! But NOT the people as a whole. Not NOW!

We know full well that the real HARVEST of our labors in GOD'S WORK, preparing the way for Christ's coming, is NOT NOW! But when everything these peoples have has been taken from them—when they are slaves in foreign lands—when they are cruelly treated, beaten, unmercifully even martyred and put to death—THEN millions of those who remain alive WILL cry out to God—WILL repent—WILL turn to live GOD'S WAY. *That* is when the REAL HARVEST FROM THIS PRESENT WORK OF GOD will be reaped.

Millions, then, will remember they *heard* Christ's TRUE message over *The World Tomorrow*—read it in *The Plain Truth!*

Then they will say: "That *was* the true message sent by GOD after all!" Many will take it lightly now—just as Israelites of old took God's message to them through His prophets. But when these things really HAPPEN—when people realize NO ONE ELSE warned them—then they will KNOW just WHO are the real FALSE prophets today! *Then* they will KNOW which is God's truth!

The pitiful, pitiful tragedy of it! This realization will come TOO LATE to save the *many* from this repeated *sevenfold* punishment! BUT, for millions, *not* too late for their salvation—for God's GIFT of ETERNAL LIFE!

Millions Finally Converted!

Notice the prophecies of this very thing! Return for a moment to Jeremiah's prophecy. The 30th chapter, from which I quoted, ends with these words: " . . . in the *latter days* ye shall consider it." The prophecy is for OUR TIME, now!

Read right on in chapter 31:

"At the same time, saith the Eternal, will I be the God of all the families of Israel, and they shall be my people. Thus saith the Eternal, The people which were left of the sword [those still then alive] found grace in the wilderness; even Israel, when he went to find him rest" (marginal rendering). Or, as in the RSV, " . . . when Israel *sought for* rest, the Eternal appeared to him from afar." Or, as in the Moffatt translation: " . . . Those who survive the sword shall find grace in the dungeon." That is, in captivity and in slavery!

Continue, "Again I will build thee, and thou shalt be built, O virgin of Israel: thou shalt again be adorned

220

with thy tabrets, and shalt go forth in the dances of them that make merry. . . . They shall come with weeping, and with supplications will I lead them: I will cause them to walk by the rivers of waters *in a straight way* [God's law!], wherein they shall not stumble: for I am a father to Israel, and Ephraim is my firstborn [birthright-holder]. Hear the word of the Eternal, O ye nations, and declare it in the isles afar off, and say, He that scattered Israel will gather him, and keep him, as a shepherd doth his flock" (Jer. 31:4, 9-10).

Later Jeremiah was inspired to write: "In those days, and in that time, saith the Eternal, the children of Israel shall come, they and the children of Judah together, going and weeping: they shall go, and seek the Eternal their God. They shall ask the way to Zion with their faces thitherward, saying, Come, and let us join ourselves to the Eternal in a perpetual covenant [the NEW COVENANT] THAT SHALL NOT BE FORGOTTEN. MY PEOPLE HATH BEEN LOST SHEEP: their shepherds [professing Christian ministers] have caused them to go astray . . . " (Jer. 50:4-6).

Later in this chapter: "In those days, and in that time, saith the Eternal, the iniquity of Israel shall be sought for, and there shall be none; and the sins of Judah, and they shall not be found: for I will pardon them whom I reserve [leave as a remnant]" (verse 20).

Hosea Summarizes It

This whole matter of Israel's rebellion against RIGHT WAYS, of God's driving them out, divorcing them, withholding the bestowal of the birthright for 2520 years—and of Israel's final redemption *after* the three additional sevenfold more *intense* corrective punishments—is summarized by the prophet Hosea.

But Hosea also becomes very concise, direct, and

specific in detailing Britain-America's national ATTI-TUDE right now!

To picture this whole course of infidelity, rejection, withholding of blessing, *extreme* correction, and final awakening of Israel, God directed the prophet to marry a whore—to picture what Israel was to God. She bore him a son. God instructed Hosea to name the son *Jezreel*, meaning *"God will disperse."* For God said, " ... I will ... cause to cease the kingdom of the house of Israel. ... I will break the bow of Israel in the valley of Jezreel" (Hos. 1:4-5). The kingdom—the government— did cease at the Assyrian captivity—721-718 B.C.

Hosea's harlot wife conceived again, and bore a daughter. God instructed that she be named *"Lo-ruhamah,"* meaning *"no mercy"* for, saith God, " ... I will no more have mercy upon the house of Israel; but I will utterly take them away" (verse 6).

Later this lewd wife had another son. "Call his name," saith God, *"Lo-ammi* [meaning *"not my people"*]: for ye are not my people, and I will not be your God" (verse 9).

Yet to Find the True Riches

"Yet," continued the Eternal, "the number of the children of Israel shall be as the sand of the sea, which cannot be measured nor numbered; and it shall come to pass, that in the place where it was said unto them, Ye are not my people, there it shall be said unto them, YE are the sons of the living God. Then shall the children of Judah [the Jews] and the children of Israel ["Lost Ten Tribes"] be gathered together, and appoint themselves one head, and they shall come up out of the land [spread out far beyond their land—Moffatt translation]: for great shall be the day of Jezreel" (Hosea 1:10-11).

There, in brief, is a picture of the whole course of

222

God's dealing with Israel. Today, our people say they are NOT "Israel." That is, NOT God's people! They think that the Jews, and the Jews *only*, are Israel. But very soon, now, they are going to KNOW their identity. Thousands will learn it from this very book you are now reading. The MILLIONS will learn it at Christ's coming!

In Hosea 2, God says, in regard to our now having possessed the unprecedented WEALTH of the birthright promise: "For she did not know that I gave her corn, and wine, and oil, and MULTIPLIED her silver and gold, which they prepared for Baal. Therefore will I return, and TAKE AWAY my corn in the time thereof, and my wine in the season thereof, and will recover my wool and my flax given to cover her nakedness [her SIN]" (verses 8-9).

But finally, when the correction becomes INTENSE enough, our peoples *will acknowledge their transgressions*, WILL REPENT, WILL SEEK THEIR GOD!

God's People — At Last!

"And it shall be at that day, saith the Eternal, that thou shalt call me *Ishi* ["MY HUSBAND"]; and shalt call me no more *Baali* ["MY LORD"]" (verse 16).

"And," concludes this second chapter, "I will have mercy upon her that had not obtained mercy; and I will say to them which were not my people, *Thou art my people*; and they shall say, Thou art MY GOD" (verse 23).

Then begins GOD'S MESSAGE TO OUR PEOPLES TODAY—especially to the British peoples!

"Hear the word of the Eternal, ye children of Israel [you people of the British Commonwealth and the United States!]: for the Eternal hath a controversy with the inhabitants of the land, because there is no truth, nor mercy, *nor knowledge of God in the land*. By swearing, and lying, and killing, and stealing, and committing adultery, they break out, and blood toucheth blood. Therefore shall the land [of America and Britain] mourn, and every one that dwelleth therein shall languish . . . " (Hosea 4:1-3).

To the modern ministers in the churches of Britain and America, God says: "My people are destroyed for lack of knowledge: because thou hast rejected knowledge, I will also reject thee, that thou shalt be no priest to me: seeing thou hast forgotten *the law of thy God*, I will also forget thy children. As they were increased, so they sinned against me: therefore will I change their glory into shame" (verses 6-7).

Speaking of the coming manyfold INTENSITY of corrective PUNISHMENT, God says, " . . . in their affliction *they will seek me early*" (Hos. 5:15).

To Britain Today!

Speaking of modern Britain God says: "Israel [Britain] indeed is STUBBORN as a restive heifer; how can the Eternal feed them now . . . ?" (Hos. 4:16, Moffatt translation.) God "feeds" His people today with HIS WORD—HIS GOSPEL OF THE KINGDOM OF GOD—His WARNING of what is quickly to come! The British government *would not allow* any broadcasting facilities within its jurisdiction that might be used by God's servants to proclaim GOD'S MESSAGE OF THIS HOUR to the British peoples!

But GOD was determined to get His message to the British!

So, the first week in 1953, God's message started getting into Britain *from Europe*—when *The World Tomorrow* program began going out on the superpowered voice of Radio Luxembourg!

When Radio Luxembourg was no longer effective for this message, God raised up broadcasting stations on SHIPS, ANCHORED JUST OUTSIDE BRITAIN'S JURISDICTION.

224

The World Tomorrow WAS THEN THUNDERED over all of Britain DAILY, from SEVEN of these ships. They were not illegal. They violated no law of man. They DID proclaim faithfully THE LAW OF *God!* But the British authorities falsely called them "pirate" ships. They were NOT pirates. They were not marauders. They did not invade the land and pillage or steal. They harmed no one!

But most governments of MAN would like to CONTROL what their PEOPLE hear or do not hear! They want to CONTROL your thinking for you!

The British government and the national Church of England would LEGALIZE the revolting perversion of homosexuality! They would CONDONE heinous SINS, but no door inside the U.K. is open to broadcasting GOD'S MESSAGE!

But God DID get His message to Britain.

God Said It! God Did It!

God has said, "Surely the Lord Eternal will do nothing, but he revealeth his secret unto his servants the prophets" (Amos 3:7), and in the verse just before this, "Shall a trumpet be blown in the city, and the people not be afraid?"

God has said, IN YOUR BIBLE, that He would get the warning to His people Ephraim-BRITAIN. He has foretold: "Ephraim shall be desolate in the day of rebuke [and Britain is rapidly headed toward that prophesied desolation now]: among the tribes of Israel *have I made known* that which shall surely be" (Hos. 5:9).

Also, God said of Britain and America: "Ephraim, he hath mixed himself among the people; Ephraim is a cake not turned [half-baked]. Strangers have devoured his strength, and he knoweth it not: yea, gray hairs are here and there upon him, yet he knoweth not. And the pride of Israel testifieth to his face: and they do not

225

return to the Eternal their God, nor seek him for all this. Ephraim also is like a silly dove without heart: they call to Egypt, they go to Assyria [Germany]. When they shall go, I will spread my net upon them; I will bring them down as the fowls of the heaven; *I will chastise them*, AS THEIR CONGREGATION HATH HEARD"—from *The World Tomorrow* broadcast warning! (Hos. 7:8-12.)

Yes, God said long ago He would GET THE WARNING into the hearing of Britain. Even though He had to do it FROM OUTSIDE BRITISH JURISDICTION, God moved miraculously to get His message thundered to all Britain.

Britain has been warned!

And the British government has NO POWER whatsoever to prevent the *manyfold* INTENSITY of corrective PUNISHMENT a loving GOD is going to cause to strike!

GOD'S PURPOSE SHALL STAND!

They Will Realize!

Some day, people will wake up to REALIZE this is the Work of GOD!

Of British churchianity, God says, "The Ephraimites are wedding to idolatry; LET THEM ALONE!—a drunken band, a lustful company, in love *with shameful worship*, not with my glory. When the whirlwind sweeps them off, they shall feel shame for their altars" (Hos. 4:17-19—Moffatt translation).

God says, "I withdraw to my own place, *till* they feel their iniquity and seek my face, searching for me in their distress, crying, 'Let us return to the Eternal, for he has torn us, he will heal us, he has wounded, he will bind us up: in a day or two [Authorized Version—after two days] he will revive us, and on the third day he will raise us to live under his care ...'" (Hos. 5:15-6:2, Moffatt translation). The coming Great Tribulation probably will last about 2½ years—the "Day of the Lord"

226

about one year—then comes the RESURRECTION and second coming of Christ!

The entire book of Hosea carries a blistering message and warning to the BRITISH PEOPLE TODAY!

You Can Escape This Punishment!

God warns us through prophecy that our sins are fast increasing. And now the *day of reckoning* is here! The foreign sword always has attacked us. In this fearful, awesome atomic age, World War III will *start* with nuclear devastation unleashed on London, Birmingham, Manchester, Liverpool, New York, Washington, Philadelphia, Detroit, Chicago, Pittsburgh, without warning! God help our nations to wake up before it's too late!

Yes, we are God's chosen people ISRAEL! *Think what that means!* Chosen, not for favors while we defy our God, but chosen for SERVICE we have failed to perform.

We should shout for joy at the discovery of our true identity—and we should be brought to REPENT—and to TURN TO GOD—and to get back of this crusade by radio and by printed word to WARN our people, and to call upon God in REAL heartrending prayer for divine deliverance.

The sevenfold INTENSITY of punishment now soon to come upon the American and British peoples is simply the prophesied GREAT TRIBULATION! It will be the most frightfully intense PUNISHMENT, and time of TROUBLE, ever suffered by any people!

Yet YOU need not suffer in it.

This terrifyingly severe PUNISHMENT is simply the CORRECTION our peoples have made necessary to bring them to the ways of living which cause desired blessings, instead of terrible curses. It is CORRECTION—for the peoples' GOOD!

As GOD LIVES, this punishment is soon to strike!

227

This book has given the WARNING from God and His Word!

Will the U.S. and British nations HEED? They could yet avert this colossal national tragedy, IF they would!

But if *you*—*you* now reading this, *you* as an individual—will be corrected, voluntarily, before God lets this indescribably horrendous chastening strike; if YOU come to real REPENTANCE, realizing HOW TERRIBLY WRONG *you* have been; if you can see yourself as you really are—as a rebellious wrong, evil person; and if you can SURRENDER to the loving, all-merciful, yet all-POWERFUL *GOD*— and make it an UNCONDITIONAL surrender, coming to Almighty GOD through the living Jesus Christ as personal Savior—then NO PLAGUE shall come near you! (Ps. 91:8-11), but you shall be accounted worthy to *escape* all these frightful things and to STAND before Christ at His return (Luke 21:35-36).

Those in the true Body of Christ shall be taken to a place of SAFETY, until this Tribulation be over (Rev. 3:10-11, applying to those faithful in GOD'S WORK now going to the world; Rev. 12:14; Isa. 26:20).

But *you* must make your own decision—and to NEGLECT doing so is to have *made* the WRONG decision!

Most people, we know only too well, will take this SERIOUS WARNING lightly—put it out of mind—turn to other immediate interests of *no* importance by comparison! That is why a loving, just, all-wise, all-POWERFUL GOD is going to *take away from them* these unimportant counter-interests, and apply such intensified CORRECTION that they *shall*, finally, come to their senses, and turn to Him and His WAY which will bring them eternal happiness and abundant blessings!

But YOU *need not* have to suffer this intensified correction, greater than any trouble ever suffered by humans.

By God's direction and authority, I have laid the TRUTH before you! To neglect it will be tragic beyond imagination! To heed it will bring blessings, happiness and GLORY beyond description!

The decision is now YOURS!

Index

Eternal life
  conditions to obtaining, 39
  defined, 39
Ezekiel
  prophet to Israel, not Judah, 133
France
  modern-day descendants of the
    tribe of Reuben, 179
Germany
  modern-day descendants of
    Assyrians, 178
God
  establishes covenant with Israel,
    59, 136, 142ff
  foretells future of nations, xi-xii
  Israel's only true king, 59
  rejected by Israel, 150, 152
Grace
  defined, 39
Great Tribulation, 217, 226-227
Holy Roman Empire, 215
Human nature
  defined, 203
Ireland
  location of one of the overturnings
    of the throne of David, 112
Ishmael
  Arabs of today, 42
Israel
  captivity of house of, 86
  congregation in the wilderness,
    59ff
  divided into two nations, 81ff
  "house of" in Bible refers to ten
    tribes, not Jews, 84
  invasion of ancient, 8
  Jacob's new name from God, 48
  kingdom of, under Jeroboam, 75
  kingdom of, why invaded, 180ff
  knowledge of their identity neces-
    sary for understanding Bible,
    15
  name inherited by Ephraim and
    Manasseh, 131
  promises of God belong solely to,
    15
  rejected God as their king, 60
  "residue of" in Bible means
    Judah, 88
Jacob
  blessings on Ephraim and Ma-
    nasseh, 50ff
  deceptively acquires birthright,
    43ff
Jeremiah
  his commission from God, 92ff,
    98ff
Jews
  first time name used, 79
  identity retained through con-

tinued Sabbath observance,
    180
  refers generally to Benjamin, Levi,
    and Judah only (not all of Israel),
    37
Joseph
  in Egypt, 50
  Jacob's blessing on, 56
Judah
  broken off from Israel, 78
  captivity of, 87, 91, 95ff
  twin sons born to (Pharez and
    Zarah), 105ff
Levi
  probable continuing source of
    God's ministry throughout cen-
    turies, 70
Lincoln, Abraham
  acknowledges God's great
    blessings, 193-194
Lost Ten Tribes
  became known by another name,
    89
  did not return to Jerusalem, 162
  names today, 129
  origin of, 8
  protected throughout their
    scattering, 114
  Twelve Apostles sent to, 158
  why "lost", 179
Louisiana Purchase
  map, 9
  acquisition, 11
Manasseh
  blessed by dying Jacob, 52ff
  to be a great nation, 54ff
  sifted through other nations, 128
  where today, 183
Mark of the Beast, 173
Moses
  prior to no written word of God,
    15
  appointed by God to deliver Israel
    out of Egypt, 58ff
Nations
  key to identifying, 3, 4
Prophecy
  sealed until today, 7
  unlocked by knowledge of identity
    of U.S. and British nations, 8
  written for today, 7, 10
Resurrection
  not on Sunday (booklet), 169
Revelation
  book of, only complete source of
    world events correlated with
    prophecies, 10
Sabbath
  binding on all peoples, 176
  breaking of, caused captivity of

Scripture Index

235

237